PRAISE FOR *HEALING PRESENCE*

"Dr. David Shuch's analysis of the intersection of consciousness and healing is one of the best examinations of this field by a healthcare professional in recent years. He does not reduce consciousness to subatomic particles or the physical brain but considers consciousness as the fundamental principle underlying all of life. Shuch's understanding and respect for science is admirable, and his grasp of the spiritual domain is equally keen. *Healing Presence* should be read by anyone who is concerned with these essential issues—and who isn't?"

—**DR. LARRY DOSSEY,** MD, executive editor, *Explore: The Journal of Science and Healing,* and author of *One Mind: How Our Individual Mind Is Part of a Greater Consciousness and Why It Matters*

"Dr. Shuch creates a scientific framework to explain the intangibles of faith, spirit, and consciousness and how these relate to healing. He appeals to both the right and left brains, weaving in science and human experience, guiding his readers to concepts of healing that go way beyond standard interventions. A must-read for new and seasoned clinicians alike."

—**DR. IRINA L. WEIL,** MD, Weil Integrative Medicine

"Physicists are beginning to recognize consciousness as the ultimate frontier. In *Healing Presence*, Dr. Shuch explores the fusion of science, faith, and consciousness and how this relates to the healing arts. Such a timely book, a must-read for *all* health professionals who want practical tools to elevate the effectiveness of their caring. A great preparation for the modern-day healer."

—**DR. ROBERT KANDARJIAN,** DC, practitioner, speaker, and author of *The Masculine Heart and Sacred Intentions*

"Once again, the author of *The Charm Carver* and *Letters to a Young Healer* has provoked us to a fuller understanding about what it means to heal. This time, in *Healing Presence*, he does so as a teacher offering a practical, categorial, and complete schema of consciousness through which we may progress from the bottom up, at each level further stabilizing and opening a channel that leads to the highest kind of love. He shows us how to rise above the limitations of rational thought and how to establish a significant presence for the grace of healing. And he inspires us with illustrations from music, art, and his personal experience. I find his integration of science and spirituality especially useful for my practice as a psychotherapist and Buddhist meditation teacher."

—**ALLEN WELLS,** BA, BD, the Allen Wells Center for Psychotherapy and Healing

"The healing that our patients are looking for is intimately connected with the condition of the human spirit. Dr. David Shuch's *Healing Presence* offers new, challenging thinking for spiritual care. I highly recommend it as essential reading for chaplains."

—**CATERINA MAKO,** BCC, ThM, DMin director of pastoral care, University of Pennsylvania Health System

"A new voice has emerged to shed light on the role of consciousness in the healing arts. Dr. Shuch's work offers insights into reconciling the worlds of materiality and spirit. *Healing Presence* offers an invitation and a map for practitioners to integrate their physical, mental, emotional, and spiritual selves into a unified whole, both for their own well-being and as a path toward manifesting a healing presence for those they care for."

—**DAVID KRAMER,** BA, MA, homeopath, founder and director, Hudson Valley School of Classical Homeopathy

"Dr. Shuch bridges the divide between science and spirit, providing clear models and helpful analogies in discussing consciousness, life, faith, and healing. Whether practitioner or layperson, all will discover step-by-step practices to strengthen attention, awareness, and intent in order to be more present and capable of creating a healing environment. I highly recommend *Healing Presence* for anyone interested in a practical and deep exploration into the art and science of healing."

—**HEATHER TURNER PT,** ATC, IMT, practitioner, Center for Integrative Manual Therapy

"The marginalization of the spiritual from health care has been well documented. In the Catholic tradition, this is unacceptable because we value both the empirical sciences and the life of faith as kinds of revelation. Dr. Shuch's book provides a detailed theory that will help many people see this relationship in a new light and work for a more holistic understanding of healing."

—**FR. CHARLES E. BOUCHARD,** OP, senior director of theology and sponsorship, The Catholic Health Association

"This book feels like a treasure map that bridges faith, science, and healing. It has solidified, empowered, and expanded my work, opening a pathway for the highest of outcomes for those in need of healing. I recommend this transformative work to anyone in the field of healing who wants to cultivate, with great reverence, an atmosphere of healing in service to others, to themselves, and to our world."

—**DONNA DIMINO,** founder and facilitator of the 'Living' Body Awareness programs

"The time has come for mind-body approaches to be more deeply understood and integrated into medical care. I highly recommended *Healing Presence* to help achieve this end. Dr. Shuch has presented a clear road map to the power of compassion in action, elevating the healing conversation."

—**HARI KAUR KHALSA,** founder and director, Hari NYC, master kundalini teacher, yoga therapist, and author of *A Woman's Book of Meditation: Discovering the Power of a Peaceful Mind*

"This unique book sheds new light on the healthcare practioner's role in the healing process. I highly recommend it to those who want a greater sense of fulfillment in practice and more awareness of the importance of energy and faith in healing."

—**DR. JOHN HARRINGTON,** DC, MS, founder and director, Sunrise Nutrition and Healing Center

"Through practices that can help anyone create an atmosphere of healing between themselves and those they care for, *Healing Presence* will transform those who read and follow it."

—**AMY CELENTO,** certified Anat Baniel Method NeuroMovement practitioner

HEALING PRESENCE

HEALING PRESENCE

A SCIENCE OF SPIRIT

DAVID SHUCH

GREENLEAF
BOOK GROUP PRESS

This book is intended as a reference volume only, not as a medical manual. The information given here is designed to help you make informed decisions about your health. It is not intended as a substitute for any treatment that may have been prescribed by your doctor. If you suspect that you have a medical problem, you should seek competent medical help. You should not begin a new health regimen without first consulting a medical professional.

Published by Greenleaf Book Group Press
Austin, Texas
www.gbgpress.com

Distributed by Greenleaf Book Group

For ordering information or special discounts for bulk purchases, please contact Greenleaf Book Group at PO Box 91869, Austin, TX 78709, 512.891.6100.

Design and composition by Greenleaf Book Group and Brian Phillips
Cover design by Greenleaf Book Group and Brian Phillips

Publisher's Cataloging-in-Publication data is available.

Print ISBN: 978-1-62634-920-9

eBook ISBN: 978-1-62634-921-6

Part of the Tree Neutral® program, which offsets the number of trees consumed in the production and printing of this book by taking proactive steps, such as planting trees in direct proportion to the number of trees used: www.treeneutral.com

TreeNeutral

Printed in the United States of America on acid-free paper

21 22 23 24 25 26 10 9 8 7 6 5 4 3 2 1

First Edition

TO THOSE OF FAITH who accept science, to those of science who accept faith, and to every caregiver who wants to partake in healing and not just treating, it is my hope that here, you will find understanding and a clear path forward.

FAITH

"Despite the vital importance of the biological and functional aspects of the brain, these do not provide an overarching explanation of all those phenomena that define us as human, many of which are not 'measurable' and thus transcend the materiality of the body. We cannot possess a mind without cerebral matter, yet the mind cannot be reduced to mere materiality of the brain."

—His Holiness, Pope Francis, addressing the Fifth International Conference on Exploring the Mind, Body & Soul, on the subject of bridging science and faith, May 2021

SCIENCE

"All matter originates and exists only by virtue of a force. We must assume behind this force the existence of a conscious and intelligent Mind. This Mind is the matrix of all matter. . . . I regard consciousness as fundamental. . . . Everything that we regard as existing postulates consciousness."

—Max Planck, PhD, the father of quantum mechanics, from an interview in *The Observer*, January 1931

HEALING

"The tissues which compose our physical form are fed not only by oxygen, glucose, and chemical nutrients, but also by higher vibrational energies which endow the physical form with the properties of life and creative expression. A system of medicine which denies or ignores the existence of spirit will be incomplete because it leaves out the most fundamental quality of human existence, the spiritual dimension."

—Richard Gerber, MD, author of *Vibrational Medicine*, 2001

CONTENTS

Western medicine grew up with a father: science, but without a mother: spirit, because in the divorce at the Council of Trent, in 1563, dad got full custody. Now Western medicine is all grown up and scarred by its early lack of motherly love.

—David Shuch

PREFACE

THIS BOOK CAME ABOUT through an exchange I had with Larry Dossey, MD, best-selling author and editor of *Explore: The Journal of Science and Healing,* and with Brent Bauer, MD, author and director of the Mayo Clinic Complementary and Integrative Medicine Program. I had just finished writing *Letters to a Young Healer*, and through their feedback, I realized that a more detailed form of the principles of healing that I had placed within that work would be a worthy project and possibly a help to many.

Some may question how my profession, dentistry, could be at all compatible with writing about healing, a subject I have covered now through four books written over more than twenty years. In answer, I like to quote the physician and poet William Carlos Williams who, in his autobiography, *The Practice,* wrote as follows:

> They do not grasp that one occupation complements the other, that they are two parts of a whole, that it is not two jobs at all, that one rests the man when the other fatigues him.

I've worked intimately with all manner of humans, young and old, robust and frail, bold or fearful, and in every case I've always looked for just the right way *to be* in order to be most effective, most helpful, and most appropriate. These experiences coupled with my own education in complementary medicine, my deep faith, and my own spiritual practices formed in me a curiosity to look deeply into this issue of healing. Finally, my love of writing, that to me is like a practice of sculpture, has driven me to find ways of expressing and explaining things that are difficult to express and explain.

This book is formatted as a "theory and practice" guide. Although much that I present here is revolutionary, I do not want it to become a work studied by scholars but rather a practical guide to help individuals in any walk of life who wish to assist in the great work of healing, on whatever scale and to whatever degree seems most fitting to their circumstances. For that reason, I have not used the more formal structure that would have included volumes of footnotes, as those are jumping-off points for scholars. Instead, I have included key references within the body of the text itself, and in the back, I have included a list of books for recommended reading.

It is my hope that the logically sequenced arguments made in these pages create an internally consistent body of knowledge that specifies and justifies the need for the specific practices listed in the second half of this book. And by diligence, I hope that readers will not just read this book and fill their heads with knowledge of some newfangled ideas but will follow the practices so as to create in themselves an inner coherence crucial to manifesting a healing presence.

—**DAVID J. SHUCH**, April 12, 2021, Augusta, New Jersey

INTRODUCTION

IN THE GOSPELS OF Matthew, Mark, and Luke, there appear similar versions documenting one of the earliest occurrences of miracle healing. For twelve years, physicians of the day had been unable to help a woman with a history of hemorrhaging. She sought out the young preacher Jesus of Nazareth. Pressing near to him through a crowd, she managed to touch the fringe of his garment. Instantly, her hemorrhaging stopped. If you have been educated in the tradition of Western science, this reads like a fairy tale. But occurrences of miracle healing are not limited to biblical times. Following procedures that would impress a scientist, the Catholic Church of our day performs forensic analyses of miracle healings that follow what we might call "interventions by faith": cures inexplicable to Western medicine that may qualify an individual for sainthood. We can consider these saintlike forms of healing to be at one end of the spectrum. On the other end, a mother who kisses her young daughter's bruised knee and assures her that everything will be all right has healed the emotional component of her daughter's trauma. In a healthy person, a trauma or illness may heal of its own accord, what we might term "unassisted healing." But when help is needed from the outside, whether it be through a physician's prescription, a surgeon's blade, or an intervention of faith, we recognize that there are forms of "assisted healing." And if we are going to come to a general theory of healing, as we must if we are going to create a framework for understanding the totality of this subject, we must accommodate all possible forms.

Healing, from the Proto-Germanic word "*khailaz,*" meaning "to make whole," is a concept that can take many forms. Sometimes it can be miraculous, sometimes it may be very simple, and at other times—most other times—it falls on a spectrum somewhere between those two. For those in the healing arts, this brings up a host of questions: What is healing? Is healing by faith just an outdated superstition, or is there some way to reconcile faith and science in medicine? And if there is any truth to faith healing, then does one have to be a saint in order to facilitate healing? Our premise will be that no, you don't have to be a saint or even a member of the healing professions to assist in healing. There is a large spectrum of healing that sits well shy of miracles but nevertheless reduces suffering and encourages healing, what I like to call "drying a tear in the eye of God." But we can learn much from the saints that will help us understand what is possible, even if this lies outside of our current scientific paradigm.

Perhaps the first thing we can learn from saints about healing is that being a saint is not a job title. "She was a saint" is not an answer to the question "Well, so what did she do for a living?" *Being* a saint is exactly that . . . a way of *being*. What a saint did in life is something else, but *being* a saint is central to all that a saint *did* do.

Here at the outset, it is important to understand a chief feature of healing. We will be covering a lot of ground and as a matter of convenience I will often cite the Bible. But healing does not require a Judeo-Christian belief system. All that is required is a belief in something higher, something unseen, that can influence something lower. If I had been born a Native American, my reference points might be the Great Spirit and would require no mention of biblical verse. Yet, it is within the canon of Western religion that we find a language that well addresses the higher unseen world and, not coincidently, also addresses matters of prayer, grace, and healing—all topics we must come to understand intimately. I don't believe that this work will find favor among atheists, particularly those whose chief beliefs are grounded in Scientific Materialism. But if one of those, so grounded, should encounter a transcendent experience that they cannot explain or understand, then there will be an opening to what I have to say in these pages. In the meantime, if a Scientific Materialist does decide to read these pages despite their firm belief that I am offering nothing real, I only ask this: Ponder this in your heart . . . *what if* this is true?

This text is the final volume of a trilogy about healing that I began nearly twenty years ago, starting with *The Charm Carver* (2005) and *Letters to a Young Healer* (2018). Each of these books approach healing through a different lens because our premise that assisted healing is primarily a way of being and secondarily about something one *does* (see *The Charm Carver*, pages 85–89) is a very difficult thing to put into words. In contrast, there are plenty of books and university degree programs devoted to what one can *do* as a healing professional, and we will leave those subjects to those other sources. It is easy to find words that tell someone "what to do"; it is an entirely different exercise to use words to inform "how to be." This book is a prime example: It can teach you *about* healing—after all, that is what a theory does—but it can't teach you healing itself. This problem is common in art forms such as jazz improvisation. Instruction teaches a set of first principles, what we might call "the science" behind that art form, and this justifies why certain things need to be practiced and mastered. For one who wishes to be an artist in this kind of discipline, practice must advance beyond understanding the science—the part that can be easily taught in books. It must proceed to the point of developing the strength, the sensitivity, and the intuition of that particular art form. First, there needs to *be* a science.

But for healing, what is the science and what is there to practice? I repeat, this book is not about the practice of medicine or the science or art behind any medical practice. Those are "what to do" kinds of things and are entirely different subjects. Our subject complements those subjects; it does not replace them. The closest that Western medicine comes to the subject of this book is when it uses the narrow, crude, and rudimentary term "bedside manner." That term, loose as it is, has to do not with what one does in the practice of medicine but how one *is* while taking care of those who are suffering. I propose that there is an entire science and art that is currently unrecognized behind what the term "bedside manner" can actually mean.

As it stands, Western medicine lacks the acceptance of any science of healing beyond the physiology of wound closure. This is due to Western science having been born on the foundational principle known as "Materialism" that arose from the work of Galileo, the founder of mathematical physics. His new science carefully carved out a persecution-free safe harbor of inquiry—devoid of any hint of "spirit"—that otherwise would have led to persecution by the Catholic Church.

The extension of this principle of Materialism into modern Western medicine is that "spirit" or consciousness can be nothing more than complex electrical activity in the brain. This presents an insurmountable barrier to accepting that an insubstantial consciousness exists and is capable of having a beneficial effect on living things, or that a form of knowing distinct from reason could ever be valid. This lack of acceptance by Western medicine hinders the growth of healing as an art. Without the foundation of acceptance by a science, there can be no rationale or guidance for any particular form of practice.

This problem is compounded as Materialist science has become more like a religion that persecutes those who question its dogma rather than simply being a tool for seeking the truth. For example, physicians fear publishing their reports of anomalous clinical experiences such as spontaneous remission of end-stage cancers or cases of awareness surviving brain death. Most peer-reviewed journals will not touch these reports. Physicians suffer professionally from even speaking about them, all to keep the dogma from being challenged regardless of the facts! It is no mystery then that "healing" is not a subject taught as a health-care science.

As a result, those who are in the healing arts lack an important foundation and so are like shallow-rooted trees that easily topple. We need look no further than the despair among those on the front lines who experience depression, burnout, drug abuse, and suicide as a result of the stresses that come from applying materialistic solutions to problems that are only fractionally solvable through those means. What's missing is an understanding of what healing is and what, with practice, it can become. We need a science of healing that includes a set of first principles and practices, both of which are not now within the canon of Western medicine. This foundation will form the deep root missing from our tree and with mastery this root will grow into the kind of strength that fosters what we will term "an atmosphere of healing," the highest form of this art.

To begin, we must have answers to a chain of questions that naturally arise when we pursue this subject. In order to understand what practices might be useful in fostering this atmosphere of healing, we must first understand what healing is within a context that is far larger than wound closure. But to understand healing in this larger context, we first must understand what life is, particularly human life, in a way that is beyond the concepts of life held by Materialist science. After all, healing can only have meaning when something is alive. To understand what life is, we first must understand what consciousness is and in a way that is beyond how Western science presently conceives it. And again, we confront an aspect of our central dilemma: There can be no accepted science of healing if it, life, and consciousness must first be reduced to the realm of material things.

Think about this: If we are to explore a way of *being*, we must be open to a *science of interior experience* and that kind of knowing has been divorced from Western science for nearly 500 years. But if our current scientific way of knowing had proven to be entirely sufficient, we wouldn't be finding despair on the front lines of medicine, as trained professionals try their level best to alleviate suffering using the only tools they've ever been given. It is as if a young carpenter was given a hammer as his only tool and he mastered its use and grew proud of how cleanly he could drive any nail without marring the wood around it. Then one day, he came across a screw and, thinking it was just a new kind of nail, he tried to cleanly hammer the screw. But no matter how long he practiced or how carefully he hammered, the wood always splintered and the screw always broke. But as it was the only tool he was ever given and the only tool he ever mastered, he despaired whenever he happened upon a screw.

To develop a science and then an art of healing, we need another tool in addition to Western medicine. We must be willing to remarry two valid forms of knowing: the third-person science that is the core of our scientific tradition, that studies the "It" by abstracting experience into theory, and the first-person science that forms the core of all faith-based systems of knowing, that studies the "I" through direct experience and without the loss of nuance inherent in any abstraction. But for the marriage to be happy, we've got to first understand how the divorce came about and why the parties have kept their distances over all these years. Through a remarriage, we will be able to answer these questions: What is consciousness? What is human life? What is healing? And what is the science behind the art of healing? What practices and what capacities are needed so that one may be rooted in the face of suffering and helpful in fostering an atmosphere of healing? This knowledge is directly applicable to those in the healing professions, but it is equally valid for those who, with compassion and intent, view their work as a way to ease the suffering of others: clergy, teachers, those who administer justice, bakers, cooks, janitors, friends, and relatives—the list goes on. It doesn't matter what one does but how one *is* that brings about an atmosphere of healing. That is the purpose of this book.

CHAPTER 1

CLEAVING SCIENCE FROM SPIRIT

APART FROM ONE glaring exception, science and spirit have been of the same cloth throughout time and across cultures. By "science," I mean the establishment of a set of principles that enable the systematic testing of hypotheses and the production of theories that have predictive power. By "spirit," I mean consciousness, an inner awareness having characteristics that are part of our common experience, but that also exhibit properties that are not bound by space or time.

Before the modern era, systems of medicine were developed and practiced where science and spirit were cleanly united. On the Indian subcontinent beginning around 3000 BC, Ayurvedic medicine arose with its focus on rebalancing *prana*, or spirit, and from China beginning around 100 BC, acupuncture arose with its focus on rebalancing *chi*, a different level of spirit. These ancient systems of medicine, still practiced to this day, were scientific in that they established sets of first principles that were predictive in terms of diagnosis and treatment planning.

In contrast to these Eastern practices, the history of Western medicine from the end of the Dark Ages began in a very unscientific way. Medical practices were based on folk remedies, superstition, and prayer. Rationality was not primary; magical thinking and faith in the powers of the Church held more sway. For this reason, it is not surprising that notable physicians from that era were also theologians. For example, Michael Servetus, who was the first European to correctly describe the function of pulmonary circulation, was a theologian. He is notable to us because he advanced Western medicine away from superstition and toward an understanding that was grounded in anatomy and physical observation. He lived during the time of the Protestant Reformation, where the Church felt threatened by ideas that challenged its authority in *any* realm and the punishment could be severe. Servetus himself was burned at the stake for his ideas.

Galileo, the "father of modern science," also drew the ire of the Church for, in his case, supporting Copernicus's view that Earth orbited around the sun and not the other way around. He was not killed for this but was forced to live out his life under house arrest. This was fortunate for us because while he was confined, he put his ideas to paper and these became the foundation of mathematical physics. As better methods of observation were being developed and the printing press allowed for new ideas to propagate, Church doctrine on subjects such as science and medicine became more and more untenable.

But Galileo was as wise as he was smart. Having been arrested by the Church, he took heed and made clear in his writings that his new science had nothing to do with the world of spirit. There was no place for sensory qualities in his science, only objects that could be fully described by size, shape, location, and motion. These characteristics were purely quantitative and fully describable through mathematics.

Galileo relegated sensory qualities to the realm of the soul and left that to the expertise of the Church. This was a good move on his part because in 1563, the year before his birth, the Church had decreed at the Council of Trent that "spirit" was its exclusive domain. It is worth noting that Galileo did not rule out the world of spirit as having existence or agency in the world; he merely divided it off from his own science. This is important to note because in our present science-based culture, there is no room for spirit except as a subordinate phenomenon produced by the brain. Galileo would no doubt have been shocked by this overreach of his science.

Galileo then, in one fell swoop, codified for generations of scientists of all disciplines including medicine that science would not concern itself with qualities of experience. It was as if the Church at Trent had drawn up the terms of a divorce and Galileo, years later, had signed on the dotted line. In the divorce decree, the Church cut science loose from its oversight but was given sole custody of "spirit." Yet in the ensuing years, Western science not only stopped paying child support, but it also wouldn't even acknowledge that the child was born. Science has now become such a powerful cultural force that it is even challenging the original divorce decree, claiming now to have authority to weigh in on spirit/consciousness. It is ironic that Western science is now acting as the Catholic Church once did, where all knowledge must ultimately succumb to its scrutiny. Doubly ironic is that modern Church doctrine is largely under the purview of academic theology, a rationalistic, more "scientific" approach to knowledge, rather than the spirit-based mysticism that has previously served for millennia as the source of faith-based knowing. Perhaps this is because of the historic connection between science and the Catholic Church? Whatever the reason, because of the intertwining of fates that are common in divorces when there are children involved, there will be much for us to learn regarding Catholic traditions and beliefs.

At the time of Galileo, science and medicine needed to break away from the Church, which really had no business weighing in on subjects that were so very foreign to its areas of expertise. After the split it proved to be beneficial to subject all animate and inanimate things to reductionist analysis. The world of science saw rapid progress in the disciplines of physics, chemistry, biology, and medicine, ushering in our modern world. But reductionist science, now no longer just a tool for studying objects but also a belief system and a lens through which to see the world, creates a rarely acknowledged subtext. Followed to its logical conclusion, this new worldview does away with any sense of gratitude or reverence for the gift of life and replaces it with the presumption that life is just "what happens." And so, it falls to each of us simply to amass whatever we can, be it prowess, wealth, or intellect. This belief, an insusceptibility to awe and wonder, leads Western physicians to view death not as a transition to another world but as an annihilation, and the stress of this plays a huge role in the push toward "heroic" end of life care. Reductionist science is also silent on environmental pilfering, animal cruelty, the value of kindness, or any other non-transactional interaction. In this culture, conscience can have a basis in morality or ethics, but not in any kind of transcendent relationship with the source of one's being. And because science claims a monopoly on how truth can be found, just as the Church used to, it shuts down the possibility that there might be other ways of knowing. On any scale from an institution to an individual person, claiming sole ownership of the truth leads to arrogance. Arrogance, as we shall learn, is the single most effective inhibitor to the impulse of healing.

These kinds of issues matter the least in physics, a bit more in chemistry, more so in biology, and greatly so in medicine. They matter the most in medicine because it is the realm that involves life, suffering, and death and these qualities are all very real to patients! As much as the Church overstepped its expertise by insisting that it fully understood the movements of the sun and the planets through its interpretation of the Bible, science has overstepped its expertise by insisting that consciousness is fully understandable through its reductionist method of reasoning. But Western medicine needs something besides its Materialist foundation in order to fully understand the human condition, something that it lost when it was cleaved from spirit.

CHAPTER 2

FAITH

FAITH IS A BELIEF in something that cannot be explored with our five senses or the physical tools we build to enhance these senses. Therefore, this "something" cannot be the subject of analytic science as there is no "object" to study. But we can study assumptions and beliefs about faith, just not the "something" at the heart of faith itself. There are analogies in science. There are certain most-basic things that can only be defined by their behavior, for example the fundamentals of physics: mass, charge, space, and time. So, in science, entire systems of thought rest on a foundation of unknowns, but because the behavior of those unknowns are well understood, little attention is paid to the "faith" that scientists must have in order to use these building blocks to construct their theories.

It will be our premise that on the line that has divided science from faith, there has been an unacknowledged "gray zone": the whole concept of consciousness. And while this concept, spoken of as spirit, has and continues to be held within the boundaries of faith, there are scientists known as "post-Materialists" who are pioneering an approach to consciousness that brings an understanding of it into the scientific realm. This does not remove the mystery of spirit, God, miracles, or healing, but it does clarify what *can* be known and this gives us the chance to formulate a science of healing.

For our purpose, faith is a belief in a hierarchical reality beyond the material hierarchies of atoms, molecules, and substances. This faith adds an immaterial dimension of increasing levels of complexity, up to and beyond human intelligence and into a spiritual creation from above. In harmony with the Materialist creations documented by science, the spirit animates us and all living things, connecting us through the "Great Chain of Being" up to God. This Great Chain is a cosmic hierarchy first proposed in ancient Greece and adopted by the Church.

It is important to acknowledge at this point that we are arguing in favor of a theistic faith, a faith with a God with whom we can have a relationship. Later, to complete our model of consciousness, we will need to bring in components of Eastern wisdom that trace to atheistic traditions such as Buddhism and Taoism. And while those faith traditions shed important light on aspects of healing that are central to our model, we can only account for miraculous healing events if we include not only an "energetic universe," but also a universe suffused with a spiritual father or mother who can confer grace.

These are beliefs that the Church held to be within its sole authority and which Galileo ceded to the Church by excluding it from his science. In our time, it is a belief in that unmeasurable something that modern science fervently holds, against all evidence, to be nothing more than what it refers to as an "epiphenomenon" of the brain.

The Bible was never meant to be a textbook on astronomy. The sun and the planets are measurable in terms of size, shape, location, and motion, and these principles are not taught in the Bible. Nevertheless, the Bible can be thought of as a textbook for a very different kind of science: a science that teaches the principles of faith. Faith is another "how to be" that like other art forms must be practiced and mastered.

At this point, I want to make a clear distinction: The Bible is considered the sacred text for many religions, all of which differ on the basis of doctrine. Those doctrinal differences have been argued for centuries through reason-based analyses, much as a lawyer would argue the facts based on an interpretation of the written evidence. And while there is a science and an art to that aspect of biblical scholarship, it is an entirely different subject from what we are focusing on. As much as reason is a lens through which to perceive the truths within the Bible's conceptual language, faith is the lens through which to perceive the truths within the Bible's symbolic language. And here again we encounter an aspect of our central dilemma: Faith and the understanding of symbolic language is not understandable using just the tools of the rational mind. It requires having what is referred to as "an open heart" or, as Jesus famously said, "He who has ears to hear, let him hear."

Let's begin with some observations and see where they lead. First, the Bible is considered to be the "Inspired Word of God," and so we will take as our first principle that God exists. Second, during the years in which the Bible was written down, from about 1400 BC until about 90 AD, there were individuals who, because of the quality of their linkage up through the Great Chain of Being, were recognized to be speaking or writing with supernatural wisdom. In fact, their stories and writings were deemed worthy of being set apart from all other stories and writings as having a quality of sacredness. Sacredness means "to set apart for veneration or worship." It is a feeling within the heart that rings of truth, goodness, and beauty, and it is not reducible to an analysis by the rational mind. In terms of validating this experience of sacredness, it would not just have been the peers of these individuals who would have deemed their words sacred. As it took centuries for the Bible to be fully codified, there were many centuries' worth of individuals who also had a chance to reflect on these words in their own hearts and determine whether their ancestors had gotten it right.

Let's now consider what set these authors apart. They all had what would be considered an exceptional degree of holiness or "closeness" to God. While there is no way of directly knowing the quality of someone else's linkage to God, we can, as the Bible says in Matthew 7:16, judge this by "their fruits." We have three ways of experiencing other people: by their actions, what they do; by their presence, who they are; and by their words, what they say. In our introduction we began with the story of the woman who was healed of a hemorrhage through touching Jesus's garment. There was nothing that he said or did. Later in this book, we will thoroughly explore this demonstrated potential healing power of his particular quality of presence. The Bible's authors gave us their words, and for those to ring of truth, goodness, and beauty, their actions and their presence would have likewise been felt to be sacred by those who were around them. In short, real holiness cannot be faked; it can only be authentic.

To write words taken to be sacred, the writer would have had to hold sacredness within. To write authentically with words possessing truth, goodness, and beauty, the writers would have had to contain these qualities inwardly. So, these authors could not be just clever or smart. They were internally coherent in their thoughts, feelings, and actions, and by this means they stabilized in themselves a quality of being open to receiving a grace: the grace of revelation. Later we will be putting much more precision into the workings of internal coherence, a kind of science of sacredness that is important for our understanding of healing.

Digging further into these sacred texts, we find that there are degrees of perceived closeness to God. Some of the writers were considered minor prophets, some were considered major prophets, and some were saints. We also learn of different levels of heaven, each populated by spirits either further from or closer to God. This is in accord with the concept of the previously mentioned Great Chain of Being. So, from many different sides we are brought to understand that holiness is not a yes or no kind of thing, but it is a progression, like rungs on a ladder.

This now brings us to what is perhaps the single most foundational question of faith. What could transform an ordinary human into someone whose actions, presence, or words would be more aligned with their purpose as laid out by God? The Bible lays out the first principles of this science. There are practices that can elevate a seeker to be closer to God, that humans can, through a combination of their own efforts and assistance from this unseen world, bring themselves into higher and higher states of what is referred to as "spiritual perfection." Among the things that the Church got right was its refinement of these practices, particularly through its support of contemplative orders, communities set aside for the development of spiritual perfection, a concept that our current science can only consider to be absurd.

CHAPTER 3

WHAT IS CONSCIOUSNESS?

GREAT MINDS HAVE BEEN searching for an answer to this question from the earliest of our civilizations. In personal terms, consciousness enables me to have an experience and it allows me to know that I have had an experience. Consciousness exists on at least two levels: the level that allows me to sit down and the level that allows me to realize that I have just sat down. Looking further, I can also be conscious of the muscular tensions that allowed me to sit down, a third level of consciousness; and I can also be conscious of how my sitting down might affect the behavior of other people in the room with me, a fourth level of consciousness. I can continue in this way for quite some time, finding new realms below and above my common experience where, if I focus, or if I use a tool such as a microscope or a telescope, I can be conscious of other levels.

In transcendent terms, my consciousness is just a speck of dust among all the numbers and varieties of consciousness living in the world today, and an even smaller speck if we consider all of what has been conscious since the beginning of time. So, consciousness refers to many different things on many different levels. It is that thing that gives me a sense of awareness, that animates living things that have nothing to do with my awareness. It is a thing that, for those who are faithful, is the source of all creation, and it may even be the thing that allows prayers to work and specific locations to hold a feeling of sacredness.

There are three main theories that aim to explain consciousness. To see if we can choose from among them, let's look at each one.

Materialism is the theory held by Western science. It holds that although we can't account for conscious experience with our present understanding of brain chemistry, we will eventually, as our understanding of neuroscience improves. The underlying belief in this theory is that the material world is prior to consciousness and so consciousness is an end result of some kind of undiscovered physiological process. This is referred to as a "bottom-up theory" in that the cells of the brain are believed to create consciousness. Those who hold to this theory cite the fact that when the brain is altered either by damage or by pharmaceuticals, consciousness changes. This theory supports the view that faith is superstition; there can never be a soul and there can be no such thing as an afterlife, as once the brain dies, all of the phenomena of consciousness disappears.

Dualism is the theory that Galileo presented and that the Church accepted: There is the material world that his new science could model mathematically, and there is the separate world of qualitative experience beyond scientific understanding that belongs in the domain of the soul. The underlying belief in this theory is that the material world and the conscious world are on equal footing, with neither being prior to—or the cause of—the other. This is referred to as a "top-down theory" in that consciousness descends from above. Those who hold to this theory propose that consciousness altered by brain damage or pharmaceuticals simply shows that the brain is more like a radio receiver in that it tunes into consciousness rather than generates it. If the receiver is damaged, it affects the "signal." This theory is compatible with religious beliefs that there is a body, a separate soul, and even a God.

Panpsychism is the latest theory. It holds that consciousness is prior to matter and that the material world is the end result of some kind of unknown process of consciousness. The underlying belief in this theory is that every material thing is conscious, but the consciousness of an atom is a very different thing than the consciousness of an apple or the consciousness of a human. Scientific support for this theory began with Max Planck, the father of quantum mechanics who, in the January

25, 1931, edition of *The Observer*, famously stated, "I regard consciousness as fundamental. . . . Everything that we regard as existing, postulates consciousness." This has been elaborated by the theories of Doctors Neppe and Close, who state that everything is made up of a combination of just three fundamentals: space, time, and consciousness. This theory shares elements of a bottom-up approach in that consciousness exists in the smaller and simpler forms of organization and builds to more complex units like the human brain, but it is silent on consciousness that is not tied to a material thing. So, while it goes beyond Materialism in that it recognizes consciousness as a kind of body plus soul, it does not recognize a soul separate from the body or a God and so is atheistic. For Panpsychists, consciousness is just a newly defined force of nature, like a kind of electromagnetism that operates faster than the speed of light.

Let's look at some anomalous but measurable effects of consciousness, or what we might term "conscious agency," and see how these theories hold up.

Consciousness Beyond the Brain

We take the following as typical of reports published in the *Journal of Near-Death Studies*. This one is from volume 11 (4), Summer 1993, where a patient who was demonstrably brain-dead later reported a provable conscious experience that was distant from her physical body and that coincided with her monitored interval of no brain activity:

> In the summer of 1982, Joyce Harmon, a surgical ICU nurse at Hartford Hospital, returned to work after a vacation. While away she had purchased plaid shoelaces, which she wore on her first day back. That day, she assisted in resuscitating a flat-lined patient she had not met before. The resuscitation was successful, and the next day, Harmon saw the patient and they spoke. The patient, upon seeing Harmon, volunteered, "Oh, you're the one with the plaid shoelaces!" "What?" Harmon replied, astonished. She said she distinctly remembered feeling the hair on her neck rise. "I saw them," the woman continued. "I was watching what was happening yesterday when I died. I was up above."

Fully validated out-of-body experiences (OBEs) or near-death experiences (NDEs) that correlate with flat-lined EEGs have been reported in the peer-reviewed literature, including a massive study published in *The Lancet*, volume 358 (9298), in 2001. This begs the question of how consciousness could then be simply an epiphenomenon of the brain. But even with this kind of evidence, Doctors Kenneth Ring and Madelaine Lawrence, the authors of the 1993 study, defer to the dogma of Western science by carefully walking around the elephant that they have planted squarely in the middle of the room. They conclude by writing the following:

> We are not suggesting, of course, that the case described constitutes proof of the authenticity of NDEs or even that it necessarily demonstrates that this patient had been literally out of her body when she reported what she saw. We only submit that such cases add to the mounting evidence that truthful and conventionally inexplicable visual perceptions do occur during NDEs, and the fact of their existence needs to be reckoned by near-death researchers and skeptics alike. We hope that this case will motivate other investigators to search for and document their own, so that this body of data will increase to the point where it becomes generally accepted, whatever its explanation may ultimately be.

If we take the volume of published studies that share features like the recent one, it becomes impossible to accept Materialism as the most likely theory of consciousness because we have clinical evidence of no brain activity concurrent with conscious awareness. And NDEs are just one of many areas of replicated scientific research that demonstrate "beyond-the-brain" actions of consciousness. Dr. Larry Dossey has documented many well-conducted studies in areas of research such as presentiment, precognition, remote viewing, and others where the individual odds against chance are over a billion to one and the combined odds against chance are 10^{54} to one. One of Dr. Dossey's areas of focus, including a best-selling book on the subject, is the healing power of prayer. The following example is typical.

Healing through Prayer

This is an account of a miracle healing, formally certified as such by the Catholic Church, that would otherwise be classified by Western medicine as spontaneous remission, as reported by Larry Dossey, MD, in the journal *Explore*, from volume 14 (5), September 2018:

> In 1952, four-year-old Anne Theresa O'Neill was suffering from acute lymphocytic leukemia. She was hospitalized in the University of Maryland Hospital in Baltimore under the care of Milton Sacks, MD, a nationally renowned hematologist. In 1952 her disease was considered 100% fatal and Anne was close to death. She was given last rites; her burial gown had been prepared and she was given hours to live. Unwilling to give up, her mother and several Catholic nuns took her from the hospital and laid her at the grave of Elizabeth Ann Seton, a revered nun and future Saint, and prayed for her healing and then took her back to

the hospital. Over the next few days, Anne's blood tests reverted to normal, she gradually recovered and was discharged. Her improvement was permanent. Nine years later a bone marrow biopsy revealed no indication of lingering leukemia.

Healing through prayer introduces an additional element that cannot be accounted for through Materialism, and that is that some kind of information goes out and positively affects the well-being of someone who is sick. This information has three characteristics that differentiate it from all the known forces of nature. Prayers have proven to be effective regardless of if they come from the bedside or from thousands of miles away. Every known force in the universe dissipates over distance, but prayer does not. Also, all known means of information transfer require some medium like radio waves that carry a singer's voice from the transmitter to the receiver. But prayer has no carrier wave. Also, all the known forces, such as electromagnetic waves, take a certain amount of time to reach their destination, but prayer has been proven to have an effect instantly, regardless of distance. The physicist Nick Herbert terms these conditions "unmitigated, unmediated and immediate," meaning there is no medium of transmission, there is no reduction in strength over distance, and there is no time lag in transmission. Phenomena that exhibit these three characteristics are referred to as "non-local phenomena," and these cannot be explained through Materialist science.

Near-death experiences and healing through prayer both seem to favor a dualistic theory of consciousness. In these cases, a soul and a prayer are able to separate from the body and have conscious agency. But how are we to square agency being placed in inanimate things?

Pharmacology without a Molecule

We take the following account from the peer-reviewed journal *Pediatrics*, volume 93 (5), May 1994, based on a study by Jennifer Jacobs, MD, and colleagues. It reports on the use of homeopathic remedies to cure illness. Homeopathics use natural substances that are processed through a kind of serial dilution that eliminates the molecules of the original substrate, yet which leave a therapeutic trace on a solute (usually a water-alcohol mixture or a sugar pill) that shows clinical efficacy: "Eighty-one Nicaraguan children, between the ages of 6 months and 5 years of age, all with acute childhood diarrhea, participated in a randomized double-blind placebo controlled clinical trial on the use of homeopathic remedies to treat their illness. The results were statistically significant ($P<.05$) in favor of homeopathic treatment shortening the duration of their illness compared to placebo."

For over 250 years homeopathic medicine has been in use and shown to be effective over a wide range of conditions in humans and in animals. Studies published in *The Lancet* and *The British Medical Journal* further confirm its efficacy. Yet the fact that the preparation of homeopathic remedies relies on a process that makes the remedy devoid of any molecules of the original substance flies in the face of Materialist science. Homeopaths describe the transfer of an "essence" from the original substance to the remedy. From our perspective, we can posit some kind of agency that is contained in the original substance that, through the preparation process, gets imbued into the remedy. This speaks of a kind of imprinting of some higher-order organization onto some lower-order substance. When correctly chosen by the homeopath, this imprint is "read" by the patient's body in a way that brings about healing. Dualism recognizes this dynamic on a larger scale as when a soul enters a body, but only Panpsychism recognizes that at every level of complexity and in every hierarchy, there is some kind of consciousness and that this can be affected by other levels of consciousness. What follows gives us an even purer model of this imprinting.

Healing through Intentionality

Dr. William Tiller, professor emeritus at Stanford University, conducted experiments on the ability to imprint therapeutic intentions into objects and enclosed spaces. He took the central stumbling block that homeopathy presents to Materialist science and eliminated even those natural substances that form its basis, in favor of highly focused intentions:

Tiller conducted multiple double-blind clinical trials of a most original kind. He built a number of individually coded electrical oscillators—simple circuits each enclosed in a small box and powered by a battery and containing an on/off switch. In one version of the study the oscillators were divided into two groups, A and B, and arranged in two separate rooms and with the switches turned on. He then had one room filled with experienced meditators who were told to hold a particular intention, for example, "for barley seeds that had been acid-stressed to sprout and grow normally." In the second room were individuals with no meditation experience who were simply told to sit quietly. At the end of these sessions, the oscillators were turned off, electrically shielded and shipped off to a second laboratory, hundreds of miles away. At the second lab, each oscillator was unwrapped, switched on and placed on a table surrounded by freshly planted barley seeds that had been acid-stressed in a way that reduces sprouting potential. The rate of barley seed growth was recorded for the plants around each oscillator and after the data was collected the codes were broken to see which plants were exposed to the Intention Imprinted Electrical Devices (IIEDs) and which were exposed to the control devices. From multiple trials of these kinds of experiments the

> data robustly supported the hypothesis that intentions could be transmitted via these devices and result in the intended biological effect. In a separate set of experiments, he eliminated the oscillators completely and instead simply had experienced meditators place their intentions into the room that they were meditating in, while the control group with no meditation experience simply sat quietly in a different room. Again, planted acid-stressed barley seeds were placed in each room with identical light, water, temperature, etc. and again, the seedlings grew more robustly in the room that had been "conditioned" by the meditators.

If we are not going to be swayed by Materialist dogma and dismiss these experiments because the results cannot be reconciled through Materialist science, we must try to understand how these results can be possible. If intentionality can be imprinted into inanimate objects or enclosed spaces, if homeopathic remedies work, if prayer works, and if out-of-body experiences really happen, then what is the best way for us to understand consciousness?

We need a new model, one that includes the rigor of the Panpsychist view but also allows for the hierarchy seen in the Dualist view. In short, it's like Panpsychism with heart, or Panpsychism with faith. In the next chapter, we will explore the first of three parts of this new model.

CHAPTER 4

THE CONSCIOUSNESS OF THINGS

LET US BEGIN WITH a basic idea: Consciousness is everywhere and in everything. And if the Panpsychists are correct, then consciousness is prior to everything. In order for us to visualize something this all-encompassing, we'll need to create some boundaries and define the categories that they enclose. Recognize that these boundaries are theoretical constructs—consciousness is one *whole*, but from our finite ability to think things through, we've got to parse it into pieces that help us to explain the phenomena that we experience. This is a version of reductionism, a valuable tool of Materialist science. But in the case of applying it to consciousness, it is equivalent to cutting apart a live human to see where the life resides. You'd never find the life and you'd kill the person in the process, but you would learn anatomy. We need to practice a kind of reductionism when we look at consciousness only because this is how our brain comprehends things, and we will use analogies in order to grasp concepts. But with consciousness all analogies will be inexact, so if you tend to be literal-minded, prepare to feel stuck from time to time.

We need three categories in order to account for all of the phenomena that we observe around consciousness. The categories vary principally in the ways that the levels within each of them relate to one another, as more complex systems require more complex relations. The categories are as follows:

- *The Consciousness of Things*—material things that aren't alive
- *The Consciousness of Life*—material things that are alive in the biological sense, with our focus being on human life
- *The Consciousness of Spirit*—immaterial things that are not alive and are not *necessarily* attached to animate or inanimate matter, but are conscious nonetheless

Before we break it down further, let's look at what we can say is true for every category of consciousness.

First, consciousness is non-local, which means that its effects are instant, without regard to space or time. Some would say this means that it travels faster than the speed of light, but that implies that it travels at all. And while it may seem to travel, it may simply be everywhere at once, eternally present, without any moving parts. Second, consciousness is hierarchical in that there are levels of consciousness across each of the three categories that we will study. This hierarchy is not continuous like an uphill ramp but proceeds like rungs on a ladder, not unlike how electrons within an atom jump or fall into higher or lower orbits depending on the quality and quantity of energy available. Finally, the different levels of consciousness inherent in any particular thing may share connections with one another, or they may not. As we shall see, the nature of these connections vary in important ways among our three defined categories.

In this chapter, we will examine the first category: the Consciousness of Things. If, as the Panpsychists claim, consciousness is prior to materiality, then the first question we have to ask is how does consciousness interface with matter? Every theory is an approximation of the truth, and only history enables us to judge how close or far from the truth a particular theory turns out to be. But theories give us a place to start and help us to visualize possibilities.

First, let's consider a simple analogy for how consciousness might map out for matter. Imagine the common science demonstration where a clean sheet of paper holding a sprinkling of iron filings is positioned over the length of a bar magnet. The filings' random distribution is suddenly rendered organized by orienting along the force lines of the magnet. It is our first assumption that if consciousness is prior to matter, then consciousness must map out and organize matter beginning at its most basic of building blocks. The consciousness of an atom would not be anything that we would recognize as consciousness, but would be all that is necessary to establish and maintain an atom.

Now, let's look more deeply into this question by turning to physicist Dr. Claude Swanson, who places the interface between consciousness and matter squarely within the quantum vacuum state. This is the vast, empty space located between the nuclei of an atom and its orbiting electron clouds. Typically, it measures about 10,000 nuclear diameters. So, imagine if the nucleus of an atom was the same diameter as our sun. Ten thousand sun diameters out would mean emptiness until we reach the planet Neptune. No subatomic particles can be found in the quantum vacuum, meaning that nothing with any mass or anything traveling at or below the speed of light can be detected. But in this space, there are subatomic short-lived waves and massless particles that come into and go out of existence and do so in ways that are sufficiently random that the averages of their interactions are close enough to zero to be below the sensitivity of our instruments. Yet, according to Swanson, within this subtle but lively state are located nonrandom elements that map out and give rise to the elements that comprise the atom. We have some evidence that his view has merit as we try to imagine how electrons disappear and reappear between two discontinuous interatomic spaces without any time lag.

Take for example the hydrogen atom. It consists of a nucleus containing a single particle—a proton—and orbiting around it is a single electron. But electrons don't orbit nuclei in the manner that planets orbit the sun. Quantum theory describes the configuration of electron orbits, which are specially shaped clouds centered around a nucleus. The math describes the shapes of these clouds and the theory states that the orbiting electron will be somewhere within that cloud *and nowhere else*, but it can't specify exactly where in the cloud it will be at any particular moment.

Hydrogen has a number of excited states, and each of these has an electron cloud with a distinctly different shape. For our purposes, I'd like to focus on what is called the second excited state or H^*_2. In this state the electron cloud looks like a pair of earmuffs facing each other with a narrow gap between them. The nucleus is located in the center of this gap and there are two separate clouds, one above and one below the nucleus, where the single electron can be at any particular moment, but it can never be in the gap between these two clouds. How then can this one electron jump from the upper cloud to the lower cloud? Basically, it goes out of existence (quantum annihilation) and comes back into existence (quantum creation) with no time lost between these events. The electron can be in the upper cloud and instantly be in the lower cloud without ever crossing the divide. The trick to this is that the electron enters and exits the vacuum state (quantum tunneling) where it exists in a form not bound by space or time and emerges again as an electron in this new and different space. This tells us that it is normal in the course of events for electrons to dissolve into this non-local world and emerge reformed as a new electron with the same characteristics as the original one.

A close but imperfect analogy to this in our "macro" world would be in the realm of crystallization. Imagine a container holding water in which just enough salt has been added so that the solution is saturated. In this state all of the salt is dissolved in the water, but any change that would add to its concentration would cause salt to crystallize and fall out of the solution. Now imagine that the parameters were held at just the critical point of equilibrium where the salt could either crystallize out or redissolve. You would have salt crystals coming into and going out of existence constantly, and when one particle would dissolve, a new particle of exactly the same characteristics would emerge elsewhere. Our observations would only see the crystals disappearing and reappearing; we could never observe the invisible ion exchanges going on within the solution itself.

Complexities of the Consciousness of Things

Let us focus briefly on this first level of complexity within the Consciousness of Things, what we will refer to as "Things, Level 1" or "T1" for short. This is the level that templates for atoms. But atomic particles are not as simple as iron filings and consciousness is not as simple as a bar magnet. A bar magnet holds a magnetic field that exists at a single level of complexity, while the consciousness that gives rise to and maintains an atom can contain many higher-order levels of complexity.

A more appropriate model but one less commonly experienced than the bar magnet/iron filings demonstration is that of Cymatics, a field of study developed by Hans Jenny in the 1960s, that explores sound waves that cause organized patterns in water or fine powders. Jenny was able to demonstrate that the combination of specific frequencies of sound would produce complex, organic-looking structures in these various substrates. For example, in one of his experiments he was able to duplicate the precise geometric patterning of a turtle's shell (see Jenny's 2001 book, *Cymatics*). This imparted complexity is a better model for us because we are trying to describe how a higher order can impart not just the pattern of a simple field, but also a more richly complex organization.

It will be easier to understand this concept if we take a still more complex example. We will look at an inorganic compound that contains the element carbon and look at the stacked levels of complexity that are contained within the vacuum state for this particular compound. As I've already said, the nature of the connections between different levels of complexity within any one category of consciousness are important for us to understand. For the Consciousness of Things, there may not be many connections *between* adjacent levels. But there will be robust connections *within* each level and the nature of this quality of connection is called "resonance."

Every individual level of complexity contains the quality of resonance, and it is this quality that unites consciousness with matter on each particular level. Think of resonance as a kinship of vibrations—a property that allows a single vibrating tuning fork to induce a second identical tuning fork to vibrate in sympathy, or as the property that allows an opera singer to hit a particular tone and shatter a wine glass that happens to vibrate at that same tone. Taking T1 as an example, there will be a resonance between the non-local elements of the vacuum state and the emergent subatomic particles comprising the atoms of carbon. Additional levels of complexity will each have their own resonance, and there may be some relation *between* levels, or these levels may be quite independent from each other. But where the lower levels do share a relation, it is through a higher-order principle that we will refer to as "harmonic resonance." We will explore that quality in great detail in the next chapter when we focus on the Consciousness of Life.

To better understand the different levels of consciousness, we will explore marble, a mineral and an inorganic compound, as a template for how higher-order levels of complexity are held within the vacuum state of each atom. Marble may have up to seven levels of complexity. These seven levels are labeled with the prefix "T" (for "Things") and followed by the number of the level starting at "1."

T1 involves all of the *atoms* of carbon. In marble, there are other atoms as well, notably calcium and oxygen, and each of these will have its own resonance within the vacuum state. This T1 resonance, the consciousness of carbon atoms, is the foundation of all that follows.

T2 involves the *molecules* made from the T1 components, which here form the mineral known as calcium carbonate. There is a clear relationship and evolution of complexity between the atoms of T1 and the molecules of T2, and so here we find harmonic resonance connecting these first two levels.

T3 involves biology, where genetic code instructed calcium carbonate to be part of the shells of prehistoric crustaceans. Over time these transformed into layers on the seabed that became the raw material for limestone. Here, there is a harmonic resonance between T2 and T3, as the molecules of T2 template into the forms of the crustacean shells by the action of T3.

T4 involves *climatology*, as the long-term weather conditions determined how calm or rough the shallow inland seas were and through this influenced the grain patterns of the sedimentary layers. Because it is an input from an entirely different realm than those that formed the molecules or formed the crustaceans, there is no harmonic resonance between T4 and the levels that came before it. T4 is resonant with climate and weather: The elements from T1, T2, and T3 just happen to be subject to these forces. Also, climatology is inherently *less* complex than biology as it is easier to describe meteorological events in terms of mathematics than it is to describe biological events. So, in the case of marble, T4 is not an evolutionary step toward greater complexity as T1,

T2, and T3 were, but is a devolutionary step, where complexity is reduced. By adding a fourth level of complexity, we do get, overall, a more complex structure because now we have four levels instead of just three, but this lack of progression in complexity means that we no longer have harmonic resonance between and among all of the levels.

T5 involves *geology*. Like T4 this is an input from an entirely different realm than those that formed the molecules, the crustaceans, or the weather patterns. Here plate tectonics drive the limestone deep into the earth on a time scale of about 300 million years, and in that time the details of the T3 and T4 organizations are reduced to mere shadows of their former selves. The limestone metamorphosizes into masses of crystals. Composed of compressed sea creatures' shells, limestone—a rather opaque ore—becomes a translucent mineral with crystals orienting in a pattern regular enough to allow in light. The only trace of the T3 organization will be in the concentrations of trace minerals that were specific to the species of crustaceans that formed the limestone and added color to the marble. The only trace of the T4 organization will be in aspects of the patterning seen if the marble were to be cut and its surface polished.

In certain circumstances there will form within marble an inclusionary mineral known as corundum, better known as ruby or sapphire. These gems can form in a variety of environments, but their quality is particularly high when their host is marble. So, in the case where marble forms the atmosphere that serves to perfect the formation of ruby or sapphire, not unlike how the interior of an oyster is instrumental in perfecting the formation of a pearl, there will be a T6 *mineralogical* level of complexity in marble.

So, with marble we've explored six levels of complexity that imply a stack of six levels of consciousness. But of these six, there was harmonic resonance only among the first three levels (see Figure 1), and the resonance of T3 was altered by the subsequent actions of T4 and T5. This principle of altered resonance, when lower levels of harmonic resonance are modified by higher-level actions, is the basis of how homeopathic remedies are made. Also, in certain circumstances, there can be a T7 level of complexity imparted to this system, as in the IIEDs of Dr. William Tiller, and the sanctification of objects and spaces, as are common among most religious traditions. In those cases, the interface of an intention or prayer occurs at points on the envelope of harmonic resonance according to a principle we will term "coherence." We will be exploring this in chapter 6.

To review, even though the material things discussed in this chapter possess some quality of consciousness, only the first two or three levels harmonically relate to one another and the total number of levels rarely exceed five, even in structures as large as stars. In the next chapter we will explore the consciousness of living things and we will see greater relatedness among the levels and a greater total number of levels. But a principle that holds true both in things and in life is that every level of complexity has its template within one of the stacked levels of consciousness within the vacuum state.

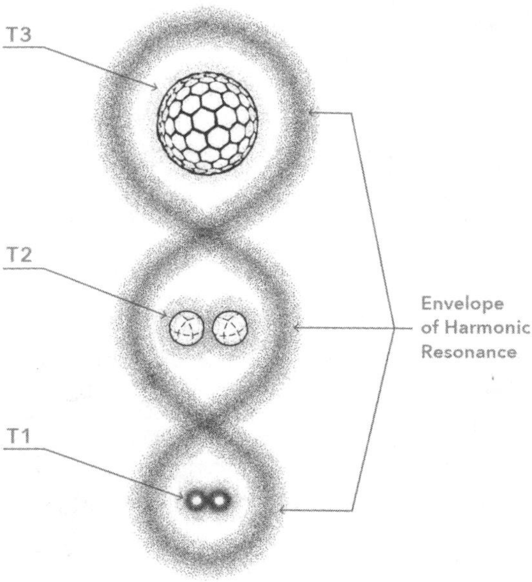

FIGURE 1. The first three levels of consciousness (T1-T3) for the mineral marble, showing the T1 resonance for atoms, the T2 resonance for molecules, and the T3 resonance for the biologically mediated crystal patterns. Also shown, the envelope of harmonic resonance. T4-T6 are not shown as they are levels that are not harmonically resonant with T1-T3 and so they are not within the envelope.

CHAPTER 5

THE CONSCIOUSNESS OF LIFE

AS WE BEGAN THE twenty-first century, the Human Genome Project was a scientific endeavor that regularly made it onto the evening news. For the very first time, science had the technology to count out and identify every gene on all of the human chromosomes. Early in that process, lower forms of life had their genes laid bare and it was discovered that the lowly earthworm had about 20,000 genes. It was then hypothesized that the human genome would naturally need to have at least 100,000 genes. But what was discovered was that humans, like earthworms, also had about 20,000 genes. It turns out that the number of parts is not what confers the greater increase in complexity. Rather, it is the interconnections between those parts that do. Scientists are now busy mapping out those interconnections in terms of their molecular pathways. For our part, we will look at what underlies these pathways as it is that *something* that relates to the topic of this chapter.

We have already seen how consciousness contains levels of hierarchical complexity that are inherent in any material thing. We have seen that on any given level of complexity, such as a group of one type of atom, all of those parts share a relation through the principle of resonance. We have also seen that different levels of complexity can have relatedness or no relatedness. Relatedness means that there is some kind of natural progression, an evolution of form from simpler to more complex, as when atoms form molecules. If there is a relatedness in material things, then these levels interconnect through the principle of *harmonic resonance*, a far more complex and precise form of connection.

Let's explore an analogy from the world of music. Before an orchestra begins a performance, an oboist sounds the A above middle C, a pitch of 440 cycles per second. All of the musicians tune their instruments to this same pitch. This is simple resonance. But harmonic resonance is much more involved. When a piano tuner tunes a piano, she must do more than make sure that middle A plays at 440 and middle C plays at 262 cycles per second. Within middle C there are subtle pitches that resonate not just with other instruments that can play this same C, but also with other notes on the piano itself that are known as the overtones. This first C must resonate with every other C in every other octave, but also with every G above it, the third and fourth E above it, the third and fifth B-flat above it, and the fourth D, F-sharp, A, and B above it. It is how these sixteen overtones sound along with middle C, which are louder or softer and which may be tuned slightly off to produce a distinct texture that creates the tone color of any particular piano, that produces harmonic resonance. So, harmonic resonance is made up of a web of interconnections rather than just the X=Y of simple resonance, and because of this complexity, 20,000 genes can give rise to an earthworm or a human!

Because harmonic resonance is explicable through the repeating seven-note pattern of the musical scale, we will identify the levels within the Consciousness of Life by groupings of seven and we will refer to these as octaves. The main thing that distinguishes the Consciousness of Things from the Consciousness of Life is that in the latter, *each and every* level of complexity is linked by harmonic resonance. To make this point even clearer, let us look at two conceptual diagrams, each representing four levels of complexity. Diagram 1 represents the Consciousness of Things, with harmonic resonance only between the first two lower levels, and Diagram 2 represents the Consciousness of Life, with harmonic resonance between and among all of the levels. As this shows, any kind of life is more harmonious than any kind of thing.

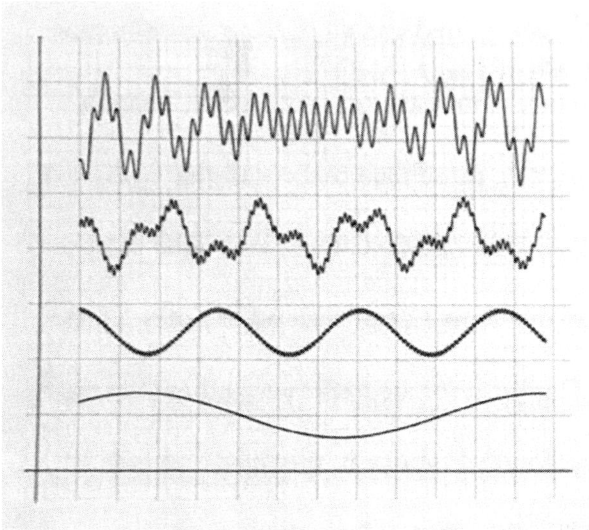

DIAGRAM 1: The Consciousness of Things.

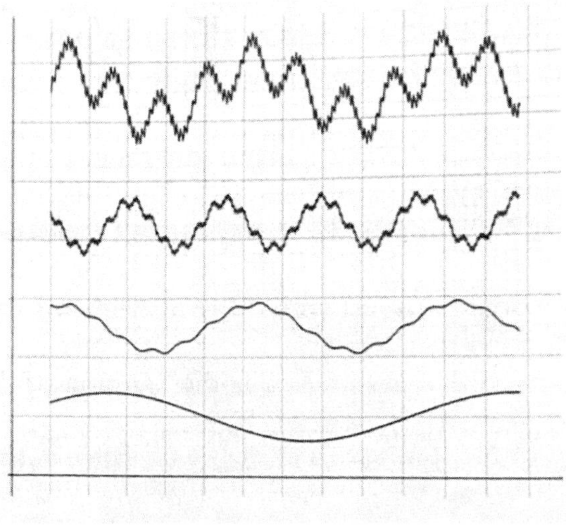

DIAGRAM 2: The Consciousness of Life.

Harmonic resonance between all levels is essential in order for life to arise and to be maintained. As we shall see, a disruption in harmonic resonance is what results in illness, and healing is a matter of bringing harmony back from where it has been lost. Because all levels in life are linked through this quality, there is always a level above that has the perspective to see what needs to be done when a disruption occurs. Later, we will look at this phenomenon through the analogy of a choirmaster sounding a pitch pipe to bring her choristers back into pitch.

But for now, imagine that you are in a quarrel with a friend and the two of you can't get past your differences. Yet, the two of you both have respect for an elder in your community who is known to be fair and wise. Each of you explains your position to the elder and after listening intently and reflecting, he offers you both a resolution that immediately clears the air between the two of you. He accomplished this because he had a higher perspective that you and your friend, lost as you both were in the thick of things, just couldn't see. This natural relation between levels serves as a counter-force against all forms of pathogenesis, so practices in the art of healing will necessarily involve placing our awareness on a level above that of our common presence, a place from which we can access a higher perspective, even a perspective that may leave no trace in our thoughts.

Mapping the Consciousness of Life

Let's now map out the Consciousness of Life as it applies to human life. Although the levels begin the same way they did in our mapping for the Consciousness of Things, there are more of them and the higher we go, the more consciousness templates for functions rather than structures. Because we are grouping levels into octaves and because there is more than just the single octave found in the T series, our numbering gets just a bit more complex. The levels for the Consciousness of Life will be designated by the prefix "L." We will now use a number preceding the letter L to designate which octave we are in. The number following L will continue to designate the level in that octave. For example, the first seven levels will be designated 1L1, 1L2, 1L3, and so on. After we reach 1L7, the next level will be in the second octave (2L1, 2L2, 2L3, etc.). Once we get the levels mapped out, we will explore a real-life scenario to make this clearer.

Each of these levels marks a distinct degree of structural complexity, and a familiar evolutionary pattern will become clear. But starting at 2L1, besides these levels of consciousness templating for various degrees of biological complexity, they also mark specific qualities of our awareness that we may be immersed in while we are awake. I say "may be immersed in," because as we shall see, our ability to experience awareness within any of these levels is dependent upon the presence of a sufficient reservoir of energy within that level.

1L1 involves atoms, but not all types of atoms. Of the 118

known elements on the periodic table, only 25 are found within things that are biologically alive. Among the atoms of these 25 elements, the 1L1 level is identical to the corresponding T1 level. The difference between a thing that is not alive and a thing that is shows up in subsequent levels that harmonically resonate with 1L1.

1L2 involves all molecules that can be found in living things. If the hierarchy were to end here, the most complex molecules would be amino acids.

1L3 involves RNA, a single chain of amino acids that enables the synthesis of proteins. If the hierarchy were to end here, the most complex structures would be simple viruses.

1L4 involves DNA, a double strand of amino acids that is more stable and more repairable than RNA, and so it is a better carrier for complex patterns of heredity. This marks the beginning of all life-forms that are more complex than simple viruses, although most biologists don't consider viruses to be evolved enough to be alive.

1L5 involves prokaryotic cells: simple organisms that lack a nucleus. If the hierarchy were to end here, the most complex organisms would be bacteria. This is the level at which most biologists consider life to actually begin.

1L6 involves simple organisms that form colonies, such as bacteria that form biofilms. These are structures that function as "superorganisms" but are made up of individual bacteria rather than a community of cells, such as what we will see in 2L1, which templates for structures such as the liver or skin.

1L7 involves eukaryotic cells: cells with a nucleus that also contain modified prokaryotic cells known as mitochondria. This is the endpoint in evolution for single-celled organisms such as protozoans.

2L1 starts a new octave and involves communities of cells that form specialized structures that also include the first nerve cell. This rudimentary neuron can sense a stimulus such as an irritation and trigger an impulsive movement away from that irritation. This level marks the endpoint in evolution of neural net creatures such as jellyfish, and in humans it marks the locus of our survival instincts and the first level that Western medicine considers to exhibit consciousness. We refer to the quality of energy found in 2L1 as primal life energy, and this gives us our sense of somatic awareness, such as feeling hot or cold, hungry or sated, tired or rested, and it gives us our sense of our body as an object in space.

2L2 involves the development of organ systems and includes a localized nervous organization: the neural cord. This allows for choreographed motion and reproduction through purely sexual means. This is the endpoint in evolution for creatures such as worms, and in humans it marks the locus of our assigned gender at birth and our sex drive. We refer to the quality of energy in 2L2 as the energy of creation, and this gives us our ability to create biologically, artistically, emotionally, intellectually, or spiritually.

2L3 is marked by a nerve cord protected by vertebrae and terminating in a primitive brain: a *central* nervous system. This allows for perception of complex body language, the encoding of instinctive behavior, and the level on which acupuncture, through its anatomy, resonates. This is the endpoint in evolution for creatures such as sharks and reptiles, and we refer to the quality of this energy as the energy of will. In humans, it fuels our personality, our gut instinct, and our willpower.

2L4 involves an addition to the reptilian brain known as the limbic brain. This allows for emotionally driven perception, behavior such as lifelong pair-bonding and the raising and educating of offspring, and the first level on which homeopathic remedies resonate. This is the endpoint in evolution for warm-blooded animals such as birds and mammals. We refer to the quality of this energy as the energy of love. In humans it fuels our compassion, love, and sincerity.

2L5 involves the addition to the reptilian and limbic brains of a cortex and, in higher mammals, a neocortex. These cortices encode for rational thought processing and for the possibility of higher forms of perception, and this is the first level where Ayurvedic remedies resonate. We refer to the quality of 2L5 energy as the energy of expression, and in humans it fuels our capacity for communication. 2L5 involves comprehending communication but yet without judgment or intellectual filter. This is, for example, the level on which a hypnotized person absorbs a set of instructions, and it is the level at which we can sit back and be entertained. At the end of a long day, when we just want to unwind or if we find ourselves operating on autopilot, our level of awareness is in 2L5.

From this point forward, higher levels no longer involve additional structures but involve different functional states. 2L6 involves the capacity to retrieve memories and to choose from a repertoire of habitual behaviors. It involves basic thinking in concrete, rather than abstract, terms. This is dependent upon the quality of energy held within 2L6 that we refer to as the energy of reason.

2L7 involves the capacity to integrate new information into existing knowledge and to synthesize brand-new ideas through a process of abstract imagination. This is dependent upon the quality of energy held within 2L7 that we refer to as "the energy of imagination." We believe that this capacity is limited to humans, but some researchers believe that bottlenose dolphins are also capable of this.

3L starts a new octave that involves a higher degree of intentional connectedness between the Consciousness of Life and the Consciousness of Spirit. This connection is alluded to in the Bible in many places, perhaps the most directly in the story of Jacob's ladder (Genesis 28:12), where, in a dream, Jacob witnessed a ladder between heaven and Earth with angels ascending and descending. We refer to the energy held within 3L as the energy of conscience. The Consciousness of Spirit is the subject of our next chapter, and in it we will make clear the distinctions between what we will term "the accidental connectedness of life and spirit" that may occur anywhere in 2L and the increasingly intentional connectedness that culminates in 3L. The jump from 2L7 to 3L occurs when our energetic structures all become internally coherent and intuition, inspiration, and the higher-order possibilities within 2L7 advance into revelation and other enlightened states of grace. A fuller exploration of 3L will begin in chapter 10.

So, imagine this immaterial presence that we call the Consciousness of Life, like a subset of the links within the Great Chain of Being, with fifteen resonant levels of complexity (1L1–3L), interconnected through a web of harmonic resonance, with our functional levels of awareness beginning at 2L1 and proceeding possibly as high as 3L (see Figure 2). These functional levels are familiar to all of us as they correspond to the sensing, thinking, and feeling spheres of our world of interior experience. In the following example, we will explore a part of this world taken from the thinking sphere:

I am in a room filled with people. Most, like me, are sitting down, but there are two individuals at the front of the room who are standing and speaking while everyone else is quiet. I have nodded off for a moment, but then I begin to rouse myself, and for an instant I don't recall where I am. With my most rudimentary awareness, I notice that there is a stimulation: in this case sound that orients me toward the front of the room. I perceive it as much through how the vibrations feel against my body as I do through my ears. I derive no meaning from the sound other than that it creates a contrast, a kind of irritation, against a quieter background and it orients my attention to the front of the room (2L1).

I rouse myself a bit and I notice something of the musical content of the speech. The two individuals speak in turn and in their traded melodies I notice mostly concordance but with occasional, mild disputes. It is the music of professional colleagues giving some kind of lecture; the disputes lack the drama of emotion except of a very cerebral kind. I derive a sense of the relationship between the speakers and between them and us, their audience. I have a sensation of the mood and the emotional tone in the room but nothing more (2L2).

I rouse myself a little more and perceive that I am hearing words and that the words are in a language that I understand. If I was more focused, I could make sense of what was being said, but I am still groggy and the words go in one ear and out the other; I perceive them, but they don't yet stick (2L3).

I rouse myself a little more, and now the sounds of words and the qualities of how they are spoken stick, to the point where I could repeat back the words as if they were just a series of sounds and do so with their "music," or emotional tonality, intact. But any meaning I derive just comes from the tones of the words. I've yet to derive any intellectual meaning from them (2L4).

Now I am gaining meaning from the words to the extent that I can follow the thought trains of the speaker, as long as what I am hearing paints a concrete picture. If the speaker asks a question, if I am asked to make a judgment, or if the speaker asks me to visualize an abstract concept, I won't be able to find an answer because I'm still in a kind of trance state. I can learn but only as a kind of indoctrination, as I am entirely passive (2L5).

I rouse myself a bit more, and now I am able to integrate what I am hearing into what I already know and respond in a more active way. However, this only occurs if what I am hearing triggers my preexisting thoughts or beliefs. I am at a level to have my existing ideas reinforced, but not where I can form a new idea (2L6).

Now at this point, by acquiring new knowledge, I begin to synthesize ideas that I have never thought of before. I am able to ask the speakers what they would consider a really intelligent question that can only come from a grasping of the concepts being taught and following these to their logical ends (2L7).

Later that day, when I am home and my mind is quiet, I am suddenly struck by a revelation that illuminates my way into a higher sphere. It is as if all that I had learned at the conference and all that I already knew about its subject were random particles like iron filings spread unevenly on a piece of paper. But in this flash, it is as if the tip of a magnet has brought all of the iron filings into a new constellation. And at once, new relations become clear to me in a deeply insightful way that was not obvious even to the speakers who had given the conference. The moment feels so singular that I remember it now, even though it happened years ago, and "like it happened yesterday," owing to how deeply impressed it became in my awareness (3L).

Recall that this progression to higher and higher levels of awareness is not continuous but proceeds like rungs on a ladder. And while it may be a simple thing and require no specialized energy to make the jump from 2L1 to 2L2, the price we pay to reach the higher rungs is no trivial matter. For example, let's assume that everyone attending the conference had a similar level of perceptual ability (they could hear what was being said and interpret tone), cognitive ability (they could understand the language being used), technical ability (they were familiar with the foundational elements that made up the content of the lecture), and experience in the field (they could make value judgments about what was being said). What then determined how "roused" any member of the audience was at any particular moment?

It is clear from my earliest levels of grogginess that I was not thinking. Rather, I was engaging the more rudimentary forms of my awareness to bring a stimulus into sharper focus. For example, at 2L3 I was like a lion half asleep on the plain, noticing the hoofbeats of antelope coming into range. Like a lion, if I am hungry, I rouse myself, but if my belly is full, I can't be bothered. To rouse in this way requires a strength not of intellect but of will or, as we will refer it, intent.

Further up the steps I require elements of my intellect. In particular, I have to focus my awareness on what is being said and not be distracted by the cell phone vibrating in my pocket, the whispered conversations going on between my colleagues sitting next to me, or the dashboard warning light I noticed on my drive to the lecture that morning. Instead, I must have the capacity to focus my attention on a particular set of impressions and hold them there without losing the common thread of their connections. To rouse myself in this way requires what we will refer to as strength of awareness.

Higher up the steps, particularly when I am near the top, I am now comparing the concepts that I am hearing with my own store of experience. If it is important to me to be able to learn something new, I must also keep an open mind and not jump to prejudge statements that may be outside of my comfort zone. But at the same time, I don't want to just accept at face value everything that is being said. So, I must practice a kind of intellectual honesty and bounce any new ideas I hear against my experience and my sense of what I believe to even be possible or probable. At this point I must expend considerable energy to visualize the concepts being discussed and compare these images with my own catalog. And if I am to come to a real breakthrough—an inspired connection between what is known and what has not been known before—I must have the capacity to receive something from above my own level of intellectual understanding and ponder it in my heart, listening for the ring of truth, despite any intellectual bias that I might have. So, to rouse in this way requires a particular type of integrity in accord with the highest kind of love.

Intent, strength of awareness, and integrity to be in accord with the highest kind of love are capacities that differ in each of us moment by moment and day by day. To some extent these can be thought of as skills because they can be cultivated and developed. But capacity is a better descriptor, because from an experiential point of view, it feels as though we have different volumes of each of these. Like a kind of fuel, they are acquired, stored, and then depleted through use. And just like fuels, they can be easy or hard to make, they can leak out of their storage vessels, they can be stolen so that we don't accumulate much, and we may use them efficiently or carelessly. So, at any one time we may or may not have what it takes to climb a particular rung on the ladder, depending on the qualities and quantities of the energy that we have available. This affects us in that the levels of awareness that we can experience are utterly dependent on our stored capacities of these energies. A useful analogy is that of an average singer versus a trained opera singer. An average singer may have a range of just a few notes, while the opera singer will be able to sing many notes and in many octaves.

Now we have a fuller view of the consciousness of human life, at least in terms of what the rungs on the ladder look like as we climb within our thinking sphere. But what do you suppose is our more typical default interior experience that also includes our feeling and sensing spheres? Let's look at the following example:

I am sitting in a chair. I sense discomfort where my thighs meet the seat because the chair doesn't fit me well. I consider shopping for a new chair but decide not to because of the bad experience I had when I shopped for this one. That salesman was so rude! And I feel myself getting angry all over again, even though the incident occurred three years ago. In my mind I argue with him in a way that I did not at the time. I find clever things to say that I hadn't thought of then. But now, in my petty, angry state, I'm getting overheated and I need to get up and take off my sweater. But first, I put down my crossword puzzle, as that is what I was working on while this little drama played out in my mind.

Before taking this apart, let's define two tools that we have for observing our interior experience: the floodlight of awareness and spotlight of attention. Awareness is the more general function and it may or may not steer us toward a particular focus for our attention. Awareness is integrative in that it illuminates many different impressions at the same time. Awareness does not communicate through words but through perceptions, sensations, and feelings.

Attention is the more focused tool and can inform us through sensations and feelings or through a mental narrative. But what it gains in precision it loses in its lack of scope in that it cannot illuminate many different things into a single coherent whole. Instead, it only focuses on one thing at a time. On their own, these tools usually work in tandem: first awareness, then attention until the subject fades and then we are back in awareness, but in certain circumstances they can rapidly cycle, creating a rich conscious experience. But attention can lead and educate awareness, and this will be a key process for us in developing the practices we will need for the art of healing. More will be said about this beginning in chapter 11.

Let's apply these tools and see where things stand in terms of the three spheres of our common experience: our thinking, our feeling, and our sensing. Our example is a typical stream-of-consciousness experience; it is a state we are in most of the time without ever realizing it. And we don't realize these states because they come about without our conscious participation, and so, we create no memory and have no remembrance of them. At no time here have I, through any act of intent, attempted to direct my awareness or my attention. Without direction, all of this *just happens*, in this case, while I was doing a crossword puzzle. My awareness and attention rapidly cycled at random among three separate spheres: in the sensations of my body where I sense tension, pressure, temperature, and so on; in the sphere of my intellect where I review history, create narratives, decide whether or not to go shopping, and so on; and in the sphere of my emotions where I feel anxious, frustrated, angry, and so on. My attention span is short in every sphere and this further drives the cycling. Also, there are just two moments, one at the very beginning and one at the very end, when my awareness was brought to a sensation in my body, and these were the only times where I was present in that moment of time. All of the other experiences—my thought processes and the stirred-up feelings—concerned things that I might do in the future or things that happened in the past. No part of this experience produced anything useful to me, yet it cost me some energy—muscular, emotional, and mental energy that was burned up like a car, sitting in neutral with the gas pedal pressed to the floor.

Let's now explore an entirely different experience. We take

the following from a report published in the book *All Creatures Great and Small*, by James Herriot, of the work of the late Grace Wiley, a herpetologist who, in the 1940s at the Zoo of Happiness, near Long Beach, California, repeatedly demonstrated that any wild, poisonous snake could be trained to trust a human by showing it respect, gentleness, and love:

> Her "taming" took place in what was known as the "gentling room," a quiet, dimly lit space containing a large, oblong table in its center. Grace would enter and position herself at one end of the table and stay silent and motionless, holding only a three-foot stick in each hand; one of which had a net for blocking and the other, a soft cloth that was known as the "petting stick." In one reported encounter, her assistant brought in a box containing a wild, six-foot-long diamondback rattlesnake, set it on the table, released the latch on the box and left, closing the door on the way out. Grace sat at the far end of the table completely still and silently communicated her "respect, interest, appreciation, admiration, affection, gentleness, courtesy and good manners" to this snake. Because she did not stir, there was nothing for the snake to target; because she was calm and collected, there was no emotional tone in the room to stir the snake to alarm. With time, it slithered over and Grace, after observing a quieting in the snake's

> attitude, spoke to it in calm tones and when the snake appeared relaxed, she stroked it with the padded stick and then with her bare hands. The snake undulated like a purring cat.

Here we encounter something like the extreme focus of a tightrope walker, who might face certain death with one small slip. For the tightrope walker there is a need to keep absolute control of his body, complete control of his mind, and a constant taming of his emotions. But the rope he walks on can never bite him! For Grace, besides taming and integrating her three spheres of experience, her way of being had to take the fear and the violence out of a deadly snake. For this, she had to tightly integrate her awareness and her attention, as these wove a cloth that connected her own inner world with that of the snake. She was then able to sense its experience as if it were her own, but without losing herself in its fear. Rather, through this woven connection, she was able to invite the snake to join her in her own calm and safe state of being.

In later chapters, we will expand on the differences between my interior experience while sitting in an uncomfortable chair trying to do a crossword puzzle and Grace Wiley's experience of taming a snake. That will speak to one side of what healing is, a side that has to do with finding practices that tame and integrate our three spheres of experience. The other side of healing has to do with spirit, the subject of our next chapter.

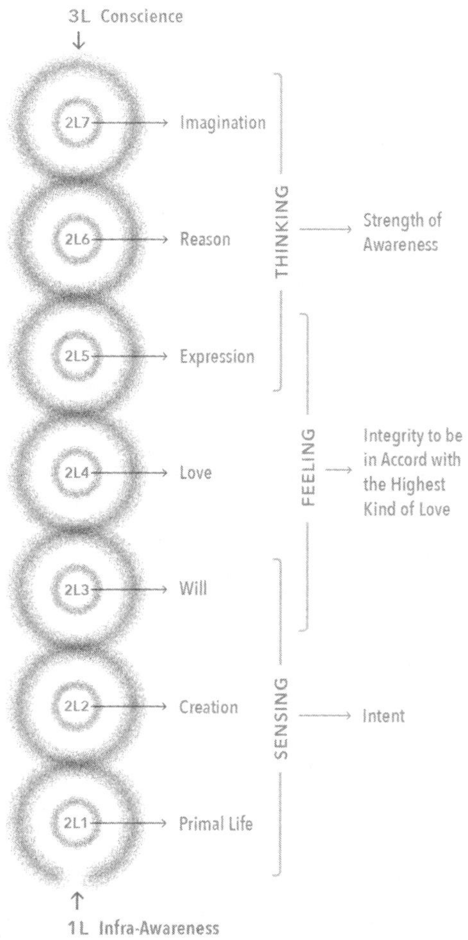

FIGURE 2. The portion of the Great Chain of Being between Infra-Awareness (1L) and Conscience (3L), where our common structures and functions reside. Each of these levels (2L1-2L7) also acts as a reservoir for the specific quality of energy indicated. Only when a reservoir is sufficiently full can we experience awareness on that level. Also shown: How these levels relate to our experience of thinking, feeling, and sensing, and what capacities, through various practices, can result from the harmonizing of the energies in each grouping. Note: Internal coherence, a topic we will cover in the next chapter, is indicated by an open channel in the envelope of harmonic resonance between two levels. In this diagram of our "default state," the only locus of internal coherence is between 1L and 2L1.

CHAPTER 6

THE CONSCIOUSNESS OF SPIRIT

WE HAVE USED THE terms "consciousness" and "spirit" as if they were interchangeable, and up until now, they have been. But at this point we must distinguish their differences. Consciousness is a term of science, centering on subjective states of awareness and on objective levels of wakefulness relevant to brain function. Notwithstanding the model presented here, consciousness would apply narrowly either to the Consciousness of Life, from bacteria (1L5) to higher brain functions (2L7), or simply to states of wakefulness (2L1–L7). Spirit is a term of faith, centering on the presence of a soul and proceeding upward to higher-order beings and ultimately to God. The scientific understanding of consciousness does not proceed upward above 2L7, nor does it proceed downward to the Consciousness of Things, while those of faith accept both higher-order spirits and the presence of spirits in things such as the veneration of relics, the sanctification of spaces, and the transubstantiation of the Eucharist. We have been expanding the definition of consciousness, and at this point, spirit, in the sense of how it is used by people of faith, becomes our focus.

Immediately, we see that the term "spirit" is confusing. In general terms, spirit can refer to any *single* level of consciousness such as the spirit of an atom, or it may refer to *multiple levels* of consciousness, such as the spirit of a tree. It is unfortunate that we have this single term that can refer narrowly or broadly to any level from simple to complex. Is it any wonder that we have trouble using this term with precision? And now, in this chapter, we are using spirit in yet another very particular way.

By our definition, the Consciousness of Spirit is that quality of consciousness that does not *necessarily* interface with matter. It has an existence independent of matter, but it can interact with things in a limited way and with life in profound ways. Only through these kinds of interactions can we know of its presence. We have seen in the Consciousness of Things a hierarchy of just one single octave with five or six levels, reaching a seventh level only if there is the superimposition of a higher-order spirit. We have seen in the Consciousness of Life a hierarchy of up to three octaves with the third octave, 3L, present only if conditions have been made favorable for the presence of higher-order spirits. Consciousness is multileveled—from the simple level held within an atom to the many levels that are part of our normal awareness. And there is no telling how many levels of complexity, how many levels of consciousness, exist *above* our own levels of awareness.

We can speculate that there likely are levels of spirit that never interface with human awareness, and because of that we will simply agree that our focus is not meant to be exhaustive, but simply to attend to those aspects of spirit that can or do interface with us. Yet another way to understand this is that consciousness is that aspect of spirit that we can apprehend, as there are aspects of spirit that will always remain a mystery. And while it is not within our scope to argue or justify any particular religious doctrine, what is a natural outcome of this understanding is that higher levels of consciousness do exist and these have a major role to play within the context of healing.

Quality of Coherence

The distinguishing feature of the Consciousness of Spirit compared to the categories that we have already explored is in how it interfaces with both things and with life. We have seen that individual levels of consciousness of every scale relate through the quality of *resonance* and that within the simplest levels of things and within things that are alive, there are higher-order *inter-level* relations of *harmonic resonance*, a more restrictive and more complex relation, that interface with the primary structure of resonance. If spirit interacts with things or with life, it does so through an even more restrictive, complex relation, the quality of *coherence*, that interfaces with the secondary superstructure of harmonic resonance. With things, the qualities of spirit that contribute to this tertiary superstructure are more limited than what is possible in things that are alive, because in things the secondary superstructure is much simpler.

To understand coherence, we first turn to an analogy from the world of physics: the laser. Laser light is always a single wavelength, a single color of light, whereas most other light sources are a combination of many different colors. Next, all of the photons emitted by a laser are aligned in time or phase and in space, whereas the light emitted by a conventional light bulb has different wavelengths being emitted in different phases and over different parts of the light bulb's filament. This alignment permits a laser to be focused into a narrow beam, where its energy barely diverges with distance compared to a conventional light source. A narrow laser beam fired from Earth spreads to a diameter of just one mile on the surface of the moon, 240,000 miles away. Finally, while a noncoherent light beam consists of short strings of light waves, a laser emits a single, continuous wave, and because of this, a tremendous amount of data can be carried by one. It has been estimated that an advanced laser could convey 26 terabytes of data per second, about equal to the data contained in 13,000 hours of movies, every second. So spirit, the subject of this chapter, is a very pure, very deep, and very focused thing.

Whether it holds something that we may judge to be good or bad does not impact on this character of purity, depth, and focus. For example, if we equate God with love, then the spirit of God is pure, deep, and focused love and contains every experience of love, all libraries of love, all expressions of love.

These characteristics of the laser are a useful analogy for how the Consciousness of Spirit interfaces with us. Readers of the Bible may recall a faith-based parallel to this concept in the parable of the sower mentioned in the Gospels. For there to be a transfer of information, there has got to be a receiver especially tuned to accept this form of data. For spirit to have any influence on a thing, that thing must be attuned or made to be attuned to that particular spirit. If a spirit is to have any influence on life in general, or us in particular, *we* must be attuned in a way that permits a coherent transfer.

Coherence occurs in two forms. External coherence is how our secondary superstructure of harmonic resonance interfaces with the world of spirit. Internal coherence is a higher-order organization of the secondary superstructure itself, which faith-based systems identify as our soul. Depending on the degree of development, internal coherence gives us the ability to choose the qualities of spirit that interact with us. In later chapters, we will explore practices that enhance our internal coherence, a key to creating an atmosphere of healing, but for now let us focus on how spirit interacts with us.

The Seven Chakras

In the last chapter, we explored the levels of the Consciousness of Life, and I now invite you to focus on the second octave, 2L1–L7. Up until now we've explored a model of consciousness that blends two streams of knowledge, from faith and science. Now, it will help our understanding if we add a third stream, this one flowing from the wisdom traditions of the East. The systematic inquiry of interior experience is not the exclusive domain of the contemplative orders of the Church. In Eastern traditions, particularly those from the Hindu and Buddhist cultures, there has been extensive research over millennia in defining specific states of awareness and in mapping out anatomic details of how and where spirit interfaces with the Consciousness of Life. Spirit must have specific points of entry, specific locations of coherence, for there to be an attunement and exchange of energy and information. The wisdom traditions of the East furnish us with anatomical maps of these points of entry, with the map most useful for us being that of the major chakras. These are loci on the secondary superstructure of harmonic resonance that project to locations on and in the physical body where specific qualities of spirit can coherently link with us.

There are seven major chakras that align to locations from the base of the spine to the crown of the head. Each is associated with a particular quality of spirit and quality of energy that correspond well to our 2L levels.

- **2L1** corresponds to the root chakra at the base of the spine and is associated with our primal life energy, physical stability, and our sense of safety.
- **2L2** corresponds to the sacral chakra near the organs of sex and is associated with sexuality and the energies of creation and creativity.
- **2L3** corresponds to the solar plexus chakra near the midpoint between the navel and the tip of the breastbone and is associated with willpower, determination, and the energies of ego and personality.
- **2L4** corresponds to the heart chakra, directly over the physical heart, and is associated with compassion, acceptance, and the power of love.
- **2L5** corresponds to the throat chakra, located in front of the vocal cords, and is associated with the power of expression and communication.
- **2L6** corresponds to the third-eye chakra, located between the eyebrows and in line with the pineal gland, and is associated with rational thinking and the power of thought.
- Finally, **2L7** corresponds to the crown chakra, located at the very top of the head, and is associated with imagination, spirituality, and the power of spirit.

Later, we will cover in depth how these chakras store energy and why this is important for the conveyance of healing. But for now, a brief overview will serve to orient your understanding.

The natural state of a chakra is to contain the quality of energy from its corresponding 2L level. When a chakra is full of energy, it spins like a little hurricane with an open eye in its center. In this state, two things are possible: First, there can be a transference of energy between chakras; the particular quality of energy of one chakra can imbue another chakra with an aspect of its own energetic quality, conferring for example compassion (2L4) to one's thoughts (2L6). Second, if aligned with the openings of other chakras, its center creates a channel through which the revelatory spirits of grace may flow through. But these reservoirs can jostle and spill like a saucer full of milk, and by this means, we lose energy from that 2L level. When that happens, the spinning motion is lost and the organized eye collapses, thus closing the chakra to any kind of transference or any participation in a channel of grace.

One aspect of these chakras that is open to our own interior experience is that of the various energies and their distinctive qualities. For example, it is easy to prove to oneself, if one has not already discovered this in life, that it is possible to be physically exhausted in the body but still maintain strong reserves of mental energy for focusing the mind. Or if one has exhausted one's emotional energy as, for example, through an argument with a loved one, it is common to still have a strong reserve of physical energy with which to perform physical work or to exercise. How chakras hold the various energies that they do will be key to the practices that will assist us in creating an atmosphere of healing. It is outside the scope of this text to expound on the major chakras in any depth, but they are important to us in shedding light on what transpires at these linkages between the Consciousness of Spirit and the Consciousness of Life. At each of these points of coherence there is some kind of exchange between our life and the world of spirit. These exchanges fall into three categories.

There is the most common form of exchange, which we will refer to as a *default exchange*. This is an exchange that occurs without our conscious awareness and we are rarely able to remember these occurrences. These are characterized by little or no internal coherence and an external coherence with only a single chakra, whereas in higher forms of exchange, there is a simultaneous coherence among any number of chakras and the world of spirit. With any default exchange there is a net outflow of our energies. These energies are taken from us, rather than us choosing how to use them. St. Paul referred to these exchanges when he wrote to the Romans, in chapter 8 of his epistle, where he spoke of living "according to the flesh."

The second form of exchange we will refer to as an *intentional exchange*. This is an exchange where we choose what flows through us, and this choice leaves a conscious trace that creates some level of memory. These are characterized by an internal coherence among a group of three sequential chakras: 2L1–L3,

2L3–L5, or 2L5–L7. With these intentional exchanges there is also a net outflow of energies, but these outflows are of our own choosing. These exchanges can be intentional choices to live "according to the flesh," or they can be what St. Paul further referred to, in Romans 8, as exchanges bearing "the first fruits of the Spirit."

The third form of exchange we will refer to as a *conscious surrender exchange*. This is an exchange where, having prepared ourselves with higher degrees of internal coherence, we become open to the higher-order spirits of intuition, inspiration, and ultimately to revelation and other enlightened states of grace. These leave deep impressions within our memory, some of which can last a lifetime. Conscious surrender exchanges are characterized by an internal coherence among five, six, or seven major chakras and involve a net inflow of energy, where the experience is of a higher force coming through us. And while these exchanges can be a conscious surrender to evil as in demon worship, in the context of our aim we align with what St. Paul referred to in this same epistle as living "according to the Spirit."

Within default exchanges we are open to what I refer to as *accidental spirits*. It is not that spirit accidentally unites with some level of our life consciousness: Spirit unites through coherence whenever there is an attunement. What is accidental is that we are not intentionally creating an opening for spirit, rather whatever we happen to attract or whatever happens to flow through us is, for us, a matter of chance or accident. Accidental attunements, like the experience I shared about my stream of consciousness while doing a crossword puzzle, flood us all the time and affect us in ways that are largely outside of our conscious awareness. Intentional attunements and conscious surrender come from efforts of various kinds that create precise alignments that are stable for varying lengths of time. We will explore these in later chapters, but for now, let us focus on the Consciousness of Spirit itself.

Structurally, the Consciousness of Spirit unites individually with each chakra only in default exchanges. With intentional exchanges it unites with our levels of life in the overlapping groupings of threes that we have just discussed. For convenience we will now refer to each of these groups of three as a "center." *The instinctive center* or S1 is the lowest level and unites 2L1–L3, or the root, sacral, and solar plexus chakras. We experience this through our instinctive energy, a capacity mediated by our appetites. *The emotional center* or S2 is the middle level and unites 2L3–L5, or the solar plexus, heart, and throat chakras. We experience this through our emotional energy, a capacity mediated by our passions. The *thinking center* or S3 is the upper level and unites with 2L5–L7, or the throat, third-eye, and crown chakras. We experience this through our mental energy, a capacity mediated by our thoughts.

In general, we gain facility in moving up from default exchanges to intentional exchanges and exchanges of surrender by developing in ourselves higher orders of internal coherence. This we accomplish through the cultivation of our intent, our integrity to be in accord with the highest kind of love, and our strength of awareness. Before we can explore methods of cultivating these energies, we first need a more thorough understanding of the energies of spirit itself.

Understanding Energies of Spirit

Through interior experience, we can be aware of seven levels of the Consciousness of Spirit, S1–S7, with the quality of our awareness being the determinant of what we can perceive. S1–S3 attune to the lower, middle, and upper levels of 2L. These interface mostly through the default exchanges of single chakra attunements that characterize our habitual states of appetite, passion, and thought. But with increased intentionality S1–S3 reach their full potential of exchange when each of the three chakras that they each attune to become internally coherent. S1 can then exchange with 2L1, 2L2, and 2L3 as a group, S2 can exchange with 2L3, 2L4, and 2L5 as a group, and S3 can exchange with 2L5, 2L6, and 2L7 as a group. Although we can't know why, as this would be akin to understanding the mind of God, the spirits of S1–S3 have a need, an attraction, or a wish to manifest through what is alive and, in this sense, they are like viruses. And, like viruses, some of these influences are injurious, but others, akin to the large DNA-based viruses that aid in the evolution of life, are beneficial. It is as if these spirits wish to live by flowing through living beings such as us, and in doing so they consume some quality and quantity of our energy and we may benefit from this exchange, or not.

S4 is a spirit of intentional exchange that allows us to impart or *transmit* spirit beyond our body to a thing, a space, a living being, or to levels high above our own perception. Think of this as the spirit of directed intention, directed question, or prayer, where we intentionally project our own energies outwardly. S4 requires not just a single grouping of three 2L levels, but, for a sufficient superstructure, it requires a minimum of two of these groupings: our instinctive and mental centers, composed of 2L1–L3 and 2L5–L7, leaving out only 2L4. S5, S6, and S7 are levels of the higher-order spirits that exchange through different degrees of conscious surrender, allowing us to *receive* intuition, inspiration, and the revelatory states of grace, including the grace of healing. These three levels constitute different degrees of the Holy Spirit as referred to in the Bible.

S1 level spirit animates our instincts, attuning with 2L1–L3. These give rise to our appetites, which show up in our postures, body language, and attitudes. We also are accidently coherent with spirits that drive our instincts toward well-known ends, some of which St. Paul referred to as "the sins of the flesh," like pride, greed, wrath, envy, lust, gluttony, or sloth, and others, such as the virtues mentioned in the Bible that require an intention to elevate the content of this link above the accidental coherences that occur without our conscious participation. Physically, the default exchanges cause twitching, nervous tics, and patterns of tension in our large symmetrical muscles and in our muscles of facial expression, all at a cost of instinctive energy. Also, postures of every kind beckon these spirits in a way reminiscent to those of my generation who would fiddle with a kind of indoor TV antenna known as rabbit ears, in order to tune into a channel as clearly as possible. Each change in the angle of my head and neck that affects the upper curve of my spine, each change in the angle of my upper torso that affects the middle curve of my spine, and each change in the angle of my pelvis that affects the lower curve of my spine, when taken together call particular spirits that create overarching moods that relate to the qualities of my attention. For example, if I allow my upper torso to slouch forward, creating a crease across my lower chest, I become coherent with spirits of dullness that permeate the spheres of my thinking, my feeling, and my sensing. This is why children are admonished to "sit up straight," and it is also how some people and most members of the animal kingdom can read body language. It is not an intellectual process, but an instinctive sensing of these spirits, and good or bad, they create wholly automatic associations rather than conscious intentions. Even traces of these spirits briefly and accidentally manifesting result in a drain on our pool of instinctive energy, a resource crucial for healing. It is a challenge to tame these appetites that manifest through S1, but with practices that we will explore beginning in chapter 11, it becomes possible to elevate and stabilize the content of our S1 to 2L1–L3 linkages to be less accidental and more conscious, and in this way we begin to control how our instinctive energies are used.

S2 spirits, the most fleeting of S1–S3, animate our emotions and these give rise to our passions and attune with 2L3–2L5. It is easy for us to become accidently coherent with these spirits as we are each like an open window and they flow through us like a breeze, animating us for a moment in exchange for a helping of emotional energy. A passing thought or a chance encounter are enough to trigger a flash of coherence, and joy or anger, fear or trust, arrogance or compassion . . . the list is long, as the spirits are many. We are so constructed as to be open to these flows that it is natural and part of life. But like S1, it is a question of accident or intentionality and a question of how we choose or if we even *can* choose how much of our emotional energy we wish to spend. Here's an example:

I am making arrangements for a painter to come and paint a room in my house, but I find myself tied in knots! Although the fellow comes highly recommended, I have had bad experiences with painters in the past, where lack of care ruined furniture. I carefully go over all of the details with this painter so that the carpeting and the furniture will be well protected. But, is he really going to be as careful as I have been told? Do I sense that he is listening attentively to my instructions? My mind begins to go through a list of everything that can go wrong, and I find it hard to fall asleep as I cycle through this list even though I don't want to. Here I have fallen into a spirit of worry and I lose my ability to concentrate on anything but scenarios that cause me greater and greater worry. It colors not only my thoughts, but it also affects the tension that I hold in my jaws and the anxiety I feel in my chest. The room may end up being painted perfectly, but if I am drawn too heavily into this spirit, it will possess me and affect ever larger aspects of my life, draining more and more of my emotional energy.

It is not well understood just how often and in how many different ways we each are possessed with spirits that live through us and deplete us of the energies that fortify our body, our heart, and our mind. A spirit of worry is a prime example of this. So, figuratively, it is one thing to open my wallet and make a purchase, but it is quite another thing to have my pocket picked! Emotional energy is of particular importance in fostering an atmosphere of healing, and so while the passions are perhaps the most difficult of these three levels of spirit to tame, at the appropriate time it is a worthy quest.

S3 spirits animate our thoughts, attuning with 2L5–2L7, and for most of us in the Western world, the bulk of our waking hours are spent immersed in this inner world. Taking the Dualists at their word, the brain is not the creator of thoughts but a receiver that tunes into thoughts rather than generating them. And while we know that the physical brain can, for example, create and retrieve memories, science has no theory and no model for how this occurs. For our purposes, thoughts are a form of spirit that manifests on level S3. These continuously populate our interior experience, and we are accidently coherent with those we attract through our cultural background, family experience, education, and the idiosyncrasies of our personality. From the moment of our arising until we head on off to sleep, thought streams run through us without our slightest participation, although they do extract a cost through a depletion of mental energy. And it is rarely a single spirit but rather multiple spirits, each vying for the prominence of our attention. It is as if we are in a river with raging currents flowing this way and that, carrying us along first toward this shore, then toward the opposite shore, and mostly we are consumed by these thought streams; indeed, we are drowning in them. We are *taken* by the flow of these spirits, and only with an effort of intent can we temporarily choose our own thought stream. But whenever we pause our effort, it takes over and off we go again. The mere idea that the mind might ever be quiet is akin to telling a fish that another world exists where there is no water. And while it is possible, it takes great efforts to gain a quiet interior experience, an event rare for us where we can actually accumulate mental energy.

S4 spirits are characterized by a more complex interweaving with the lower, upper, and on occasion the middle level of life, in that they only manifest when attunements can occur on at least these two levels simultaneously. This is the level of spirit for directed intention or prayer. The difference between intention and prayer is that intention is the approach of the Panpsychist and so, it is atheistic. This can color directed intention as without recognizing a hierarchy above humankind there can be no true sense of humility, and so intention easily pairs with arrogance. In fairness, a person of faith may pray with an air of spiritual elitism, which is also a form of arrogance, but at least in that case there is the possibility that this might trigger remorse. This is particularly important because as we shall see, there is nothing that opposes healing as thoroughly and as completely as does arrogance. Both of these approaches accept that consciousness can be directed to effect change. While S1–S3 consist largely of accidental coherences, S4 is on a higher rung on the ladder, toward greater intentionality. Science is quite clear that intentionality and prayer both positively affect biological systems. What then can make one person's effort more effective and another person's less so?

Going back to Dr. Tiller's research, the intention devices that accelerated the growth of the stressed barley seeds were those that were meditated on by "experienced meditators." Let's explore what that typically means in terms of qualities that we have already touched upon. We each can become aware of three spheres of interior experience: our sensing, our feeling, and our thinking. In this chapter we have already outlined three levels of spirit—S1, S2, and S3—that animate our instinctive/sensing sphere, our feeling sphere, and our thinking sphere. A meditator will first have to deal with quieting the tensions in their body and, through practice, quieting their busy mind. There may or may not be instruction or value placed on quieting the passions, but if there has been, it most likely is stressed only in terms of making sure that the passions don't interfere with the quieting of the mind. Typically, it is only through a discipline different from quiet meditation, such as martial arts training, that emphasis is placed on not just quieting but also *taming* the appetites, and it is only through a religious or spiritual discipline such as silent retreat or service that emphasis is placed on not just quieting but also *taming* the passions.

So, in Dr. Tiller's research we see that internal coherence confined to the thinking and the sensing spheres is the minimum requirement sufficient to *transmit* a spirit that can heal damaged barley seeds, and he developed the science to prove it. As a control, he also developed the science to prove that if both of these conditions are not met, there would be no such effect. Using terms that we introduced earlier, we can say that the minimum requirement to transmit spirit either through intentionality or prayer are the qualities of *intent* and *strength of awareness* above some minimum threshold. And knowing that the passions are the most difficult to tame, we are fortunate that healing, at least of a very simple kind, can be brought to bear even in the absence of all but a token contribution from the feeling sphere.

S4 is a vehicle for projecting our own energies for healing as in the branch of Chinese medicine known as External Qigong. Yet, it is only when the feeling sphere is fully engaged and intended toward a particular aim that the capacity for healing can reach its highest plane. This is possible through higher degrees of internal coherence that raise our awareness up to 3L and link us to the spirits of conscious surrender: S5, S6, or S7. S4 can then be likened to what atmospheric scientists refer to as a "leader," the first stage of a lightning strike. It is not the stage we see; it is a stage where charged particles in the atmosphere are forming a pathway from cloud to earth and once formed, the visible and more powerful return stroke creates the classic lightning bolt with a clap of thunder. S4, as a prayer up to heaven, creates the pathway for something higher to descend in return.

But here, for the sake of completeness, we must go deeper into this analogy as prior to prayer being a leader and S5–S7 being the return stroke, we first have a more subtle leader coming down from heaven for which then prayer is the return stroke. This first leader is our *conscience,* the energy of 3L, that "still, small voice" spoken of in 1 Kings 19:12. Conscience can be likened to the rhythmic dripping of water off a leaf after a rain, while the spirits of S5, S6, and S7 can be likened to a trickle, a stream, and a torrent. There is always a steady dripping of conscience coming into us from above. We may ignore it or even erect barriers so that we aren't aware of it, but it is the first leader. All true and authentic prayers or intentions follow the pathway of conscience to heaven. It is then that prayer itself serves as the leader for the return stroke of intuition, inspiration, revelation, and grace. This is Jacob's ladder in action: conscience descending, prayer ascending, and grace descending.

We will now look at the most intentional levels of the Consciousness of Spirit: those that we intentionally open ourselves up to so that we may *receive* spirit from above. This can be intellectually problematic for atheists where the concept "from above" is meaningless. In Dr. Tiller's work, we saw that to transmit spirit, it took the integration of two of our three spheres, our thinking and our sensing, to become coherent with S4. Intentionally *received* spirit also requires integration of at least two of our spheres, one of which must be our feeling sphere: S5 is coherent with the integration of the sensing and feeling spheres and is associated with intuition, S6 is coherent with the integration of the feeling and thinking spheres and is associated with inspiration, and S7 is coherent with the integration of all three of our spheres and is associated with revelation and various other states of grace.

To best understand this, we must go back to our analogy of the laser and in particular to the receiving apparatus for this very coherent signal. As previously said, shining an information-heavy laser beam on bare ground will transmit nothing of its vast content; it will only produce a bright spot of light. The ground or, in this case, the soul must itself be made coherent so as to be intentionally attuned to whatever spirit we wish to attune to. We learned that for the Consciousness of Life a primary superstructure of resonance serves as the base onto which the secondary superstructure of harmonic resonance forms. For spirit, this secondary superstructure serves as the base onto which a tertiary superstructure of external coherence forms, and the qualities of our exchanges with spirit are determined by the degree to which we have created an internal coherence within this secondary superstructure. This means that our leverage over which levels of S1–S7 we can attune to comes from the taming of our sensing, feeling, and thinking spheres, rendering us more internally coherent.

Let us now explore the highest states, the levels of S5–S7: receiving spirit through intuition, inspiration, and the revelatory states of grace. In Thomas Aquinas's time, it was accepted that there are two modes of knowing, by reason and the deductive capacity of the mind, or by a direct supernatural apprehension where knowledge gained is not deducible from existing knowledge. This whole concept is viewed as nonsense by Western Materialist science, yet from the collective wisdom of humankind's interior experience, we have a sense that these levels or states are not a matter of imagination. Going back to our example of biblical authors possessing sacredness as a condition of their writings being sacred, they would have had to maintain a high degree of internal coherence in order to be open to grace, what we would identify as an external coherence between 3L and S7: a coherence among thoughts, feelings, and actions, all with an intention or prayer to consciously surrender to the highest of realms.

Intent, strength of awareness, and integrity to be in accord with the highest kind of love are the capacities of instinctive energy, mental energy, and emotional energy when these have been refined through internal coherence. Then, default exchanges become few, intentional exchanges become frequent, and conscious surrender exchanges become possible. In general, our capacities for these qualities vary moment by moment, and so it is common for us to experience an ebb and flow among S5, S6, and S7. In climbing the ladder from S5 to S7, there are increasingly stringent coherence requirements as more of our capacities need to be coherent among themselves at the same time. This explains why intuition is rarer than common instinct, inspiration is rarer than common feeling, and revelation is rarer than common thought and the rarest of the three. But if we can strengthen these capacities, we can stabilize our experiences of inspiration, intuition, revelation, and other states of grace. For example, in my experience at the professional lecture, I had a revelation that had to do with an entirely new way of envisioning a set of problems in my field of expertise, which pointed out some unique solutions. This required a knowledge base on my part, but also an intent to find new answers, an integrity to pursue the truth wherever it led, and an openness to new possibilities. In short, I was ready, willing, and able to perceive something completely new. My revelation was not of the sacred kind; it was simpler than that. But this illustrates the parameters of what makes this possible.

Let us now close this chapter with a bit of insight about states of grace. A functioning trio of intent, strength of awareness, and integrity to be in accord with the highest kind of love forms the basis of a vessel that can receive something sacred. The strengths of these forces and the degree of their coherence are what set the stage for what can come through. Let's look at an analogy again from the world of physics.

If you wish to contain a liquid, all you need is a container like a water glass. If you wish to contain something more rarified, such as a gas, you'll need a more complex container, some kind of vessel that holds pressure and that can be sealed closed before the gas you pump into it escapes. In both of these cases some kind of physical structure is all that you'll need to contain these substances. But there is another state of matter known as a plasma. And to contain a plasma, you can't use a water glass or an airtight vessel, but you've got to structure a magnetic field into a kind of energetic vessel. Plasmas are hot, and some are so hot that they would melt any physical structure that you could come up with. So, to handle a plasma, you've got to hold it inside a specially structured energetic field. Spirit is like this. It isn't hot, but it is exceedingly fine, so that no physical structure can directly interface with it. Instead, it needs a structure formed from the Consciousness of Life that has been made to be coherent with particular spirits, and it is here that we need to explore the concept of atmospheres.

The sum total of S1–S7 interactions with our various 2L and possible 3L levels produces an atmosphere that surrounds each of us. There are techniques for photographing aspects of this, and some people can see aspects of this, and that may be useful for scientific inquiry, but it is far more useful and far more common to be able to sense instinctively and feel emotionally the "fruits" of these atmospheres. In addition, there are atmospheres that have been imbued into spaces and objects as we saw in Dr. Tiller's research, and we will touch on those again in chapter 8. Let us take a few extremes to illustrate this point.

If you have ever been near someone who holds criminal or predatory intent, you may feel a cold shudder down your spine. If you have ever been around someone having a violent episode, your instinct may key you in to danger. On the other hand, if you have ever been around a deeply religious or spiritual person, there is an air of peace and compassion around them that you can feel in your heart. In terms of spaces, if you have ever been in a room where a crime had been committed, there is an unmistakable feeling in that space. Likewise, if you have ever been to a site of religious pilgrimage, there is a very different but equally distinct feeling present there, a manifestation of not just the atmosphere of one sacred individual but also the effects how people who have been similarly engaged have contributed to the formation of a "super atmosphere" with far more strength in its coherence. This was mentioned in the Gospel of Matthew 18:20: "For where two or three are gathered in my name, I am in the midst of them." These are the manifestations of the spirits that are drawn to and circle around us and the spaces we regularly occupy, creating an atmosphere. It is this that we are aiming to refine into a healing presence and for that we must be open to the grace of healing.

Grace, according to religious tradition, is the unmerited favor of God, and the term "unmerited" has been fought over by those of different faiths for centuries. Even in biblical times, St. Paul wrote of the conflict between faith and works, and the Gospels speak of the sisters Mary and Martha as exemplifying these two extremes. Our aim is to steer clear of this doctrinal debate and focus instead on our model of consciousness. In doing so, we see that while the nature of what we wish to receive is an unmerited gift that we do not and could not work to earn, there is much that we must do to prepare ourselves to be a receptive vessel. Augustin Poulain, writing in *The Graces of Interior Prayer*, said, "We can dispose ourselves to receive grace, but we are powerless to produce it." A well-constructed vessel then becomes a powerful attractant, a lightning rod for grace, which may then flow through us. The grace of healing is one of nine spiritual gifts mentioned in the Bible, and it is not first on the list but fourth, after wisdom, knowledge, and faith. So, we are not striving for the top gift, and hopefully this can encourage us in humbleness! Soon, we'll need to come to an understanding of what healing is, but first we must get clearer about the nature of human life itself.

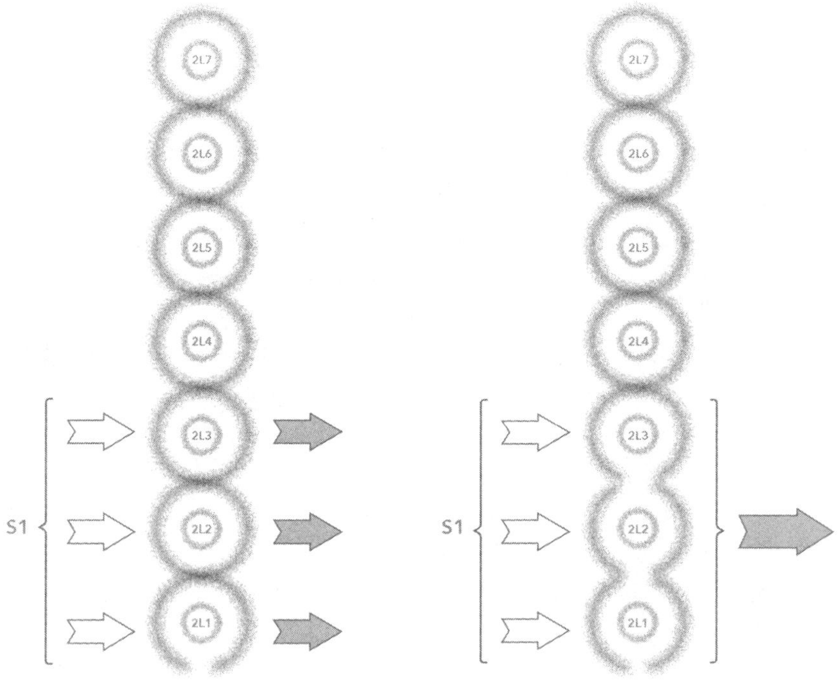

FIGURE 3 (left). Schematic of the first level of spirit, S1, that interfaces with human life, flowing through and gaining energy from our levels 2L1–2L3. These result in the experiences of our appetites. In our default states we lose energy from these interactions, but with increased awareness we may choose what flows through us and thus what we spend our instinctive energy on.

FIGURE 4 (right). Schematic of the energetic changes that come with the development of internal coherence between levels 2L1–2L3 (open channels in the envelope of harmonic resonance). Through practices of increased intentionality, these levels accumulate the energy needed to form internal coherence, which allows these three levels to function as one, enabling us to choose with intent what appetites flow through us.

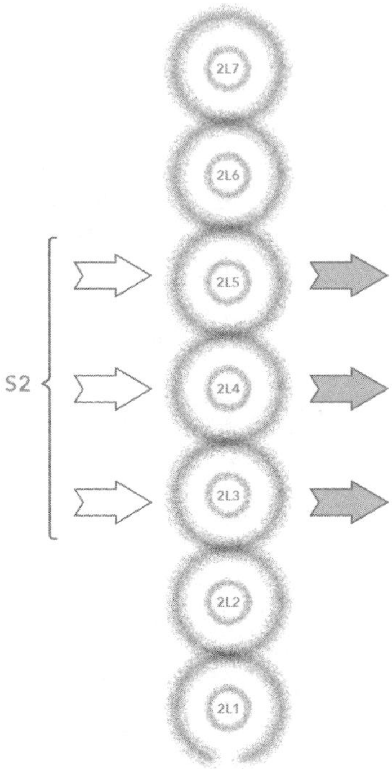

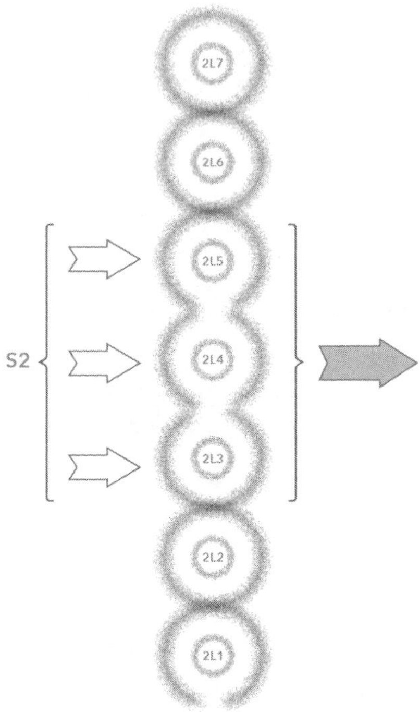

FIGURE 5 (left). Schematic of the second level of spirit, S2, that interfaces with human life, flowing through and gaining energy from our levels 2L3-2L5. These result in the experiences of our passions. In our default states we lose energy from these interactions, but with increased awareness we may choose what flows through us and what we spend our emotional energy on.

FIGURE 6 (right). Schematic of the energetic changes that come with the development of internal coherence between levels 2L3-2L5 (open channels in the envelope of harmonic resonance). Through practices of increased integrity these levels accumulate the energy needed to form internal coherence, which allows these three levels to function as one, enabling us to choose with integrity in accord with the highest kind of love what passions flow through us.

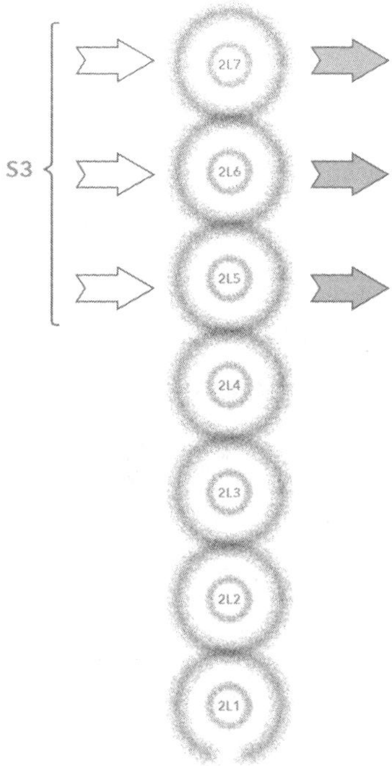

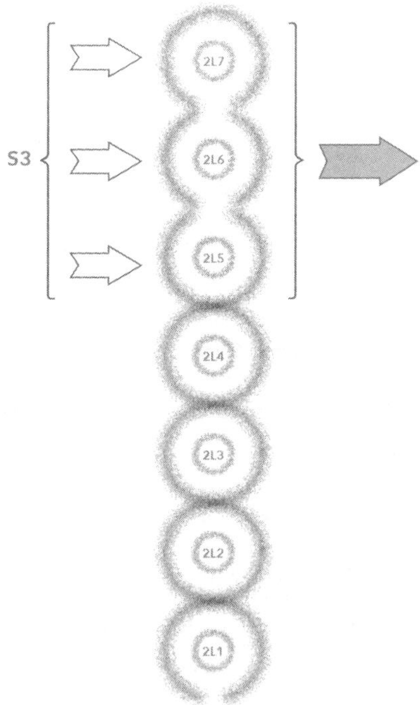

FIGURE 7 (left). Schematic of the third level of spirit, S3, that interfaces with human life, flowing through and gaining energy from our levels 2L5–2L7. These result in the experiences of our thoughts. In our default states we lose energy from these interactions, but with increased awareness we may choose what flows through us and what we spend our mental energy on.

FIGURE 8 (right). Schematic of the energetic changes that come with the development of internal coherence between levels 2L5–2L7 (open channels in the envelope of harmonic resonance). Through practices of increased awareness these levels accumulate the energy needed to form internal coherence, which allows these three levels to function as one, enabling us to choose with our strength of awareness what thoughts flow through us.

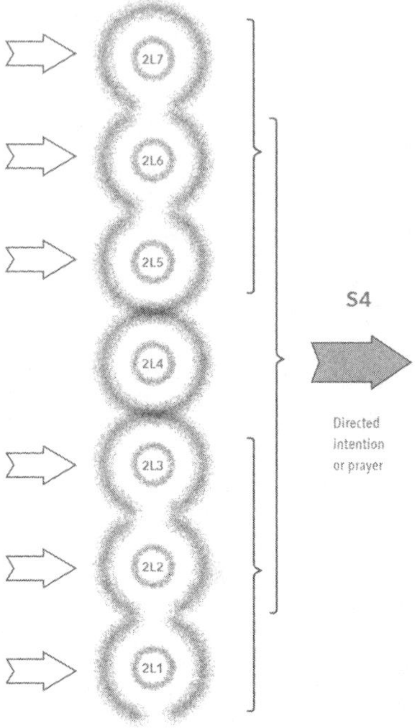

FIGURE 9. Schematic of the fourth level of spirit, S4, that interfaces with human life. From this level forward, there is no default exchange, no accidental attunements. This is the first state that arises solely from our own intention. It is the basis for directed prayer. It requires internal coherence in both the thinking and sensing spheres, but only reaches its highest possibility when there is also coherence with the feeling sphere.

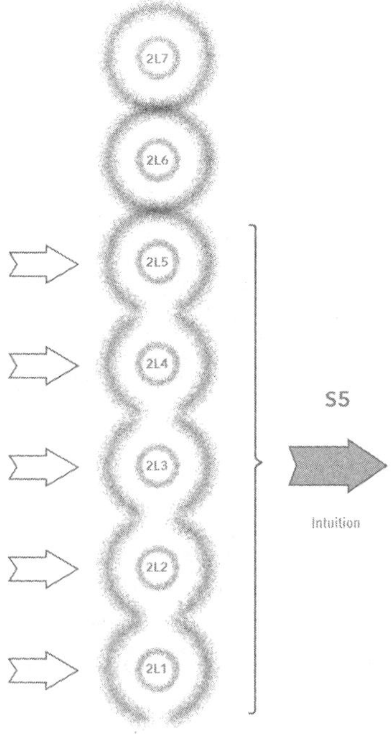

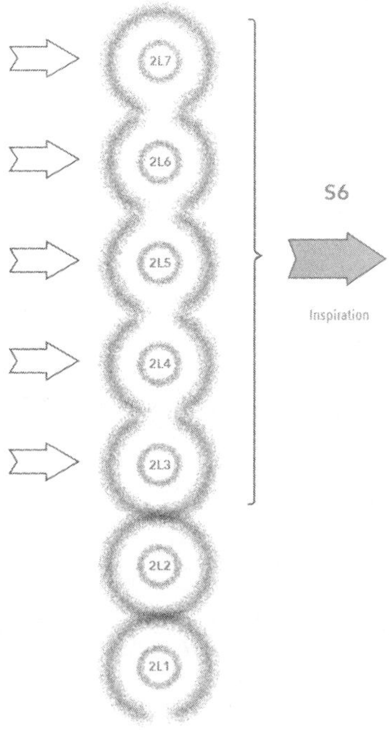

FIGURE 10 (left). Schematic of the fifth level of spirit, S5, that interfaces with human life through intentional exchange. This is the level where internal coherences have been established between all the levels of the sensing and feeling spheres (2L1-2L5), and this gives rise to the possibility of receiving intuition.

FIGURE 11 (right). Schematic of the sixth level of spirit, S6, that interfaces with human life through intentional exchange. This is the level where internal coherences have been established between all the levels of the feeling and thinking spheres (2L3-2L7), and this gives rise to the possibility of receiving inspiration.

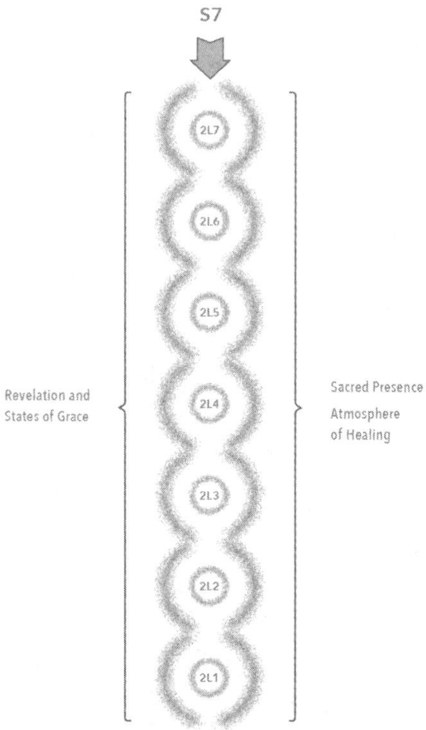

FIGURE 12. Schematic of the seventh level of spirit, S7, that interfaces with human life through conscious surrender. When 2L1-2L7 are all internally coherent and "speak with one voice," the channel between 2L7 and 3L opens and we then dispose ourselves to receive various states of grace. This is the only level where our interaction with spirit does not result in a net loss of our energy as here, we become a channel; there is a higher energy flowing through us. The only cost to us is in maintaining our internal coherences.

CHAPTER 7

WHAT IS HUMAN LIFE?

HUMAN LIFE AS DEFINED by science is profoundly different from human life as defined by faith. Because our model includes faith, we must begin by exploring the concept of purpose. Purpose has a narrow meaning in science because science is only interested in material outcomes. We eat and eliminate in order to grow, we perceive through our senses in order to survive, and we pair-bond in order to reproduce. But our premise is that not only does life have purpose, but just as each level of complexity has its own spirit, each also has one or more purposes, although these may be largely unknowable to us. And while this book is not meant to be a treatise on this subject, we must touch on three levels of complexity to cover those that are key to our understanding of healing.

On 2L1–L5, the level of our physical body—a level that we share with much of organic life—we are machines that transform simple forms of matter into more complex forms of matter. We breathe, we extract elements from the air, and we exhale what we cannot use. In this way, we are a party to raising up the Consciousness of Things in the air to the Consciousness of Life. We eat and extract substances from our food and excrete what we cannot use and, in this way, we raise up the levels of complexity of what we eat by taking simpler life-forms and making them part of us. Further, through a combination of good habits and certain forms of discipline, we can build up the energies of these instinctive functions and create a reserve of what Chinese medicine calls *chi* and what homeopathic medicine calls our *vital force*.

But as much as we are part of an evolutionary process, we are equally part of a devolutionary process as inevitably our physical bodies break down and die. In that return arc, in the absence of an impulse of healing and sufficient vital force, our harmonic resonances fray, setting the stage for degradation by simpler life-forms. For fungi, bacteria, insects, and carnivores, our complex material structures serve as food for their own simpler structures. On this most basic level, we are part of a cycle of organic life: We emerge from it with at least fourteen levels of complexity and, in time, we become food for lower life-forms, and thus our bodies return to dust. If there are higher purposes for this cycle of organic life, what might any of them be?

Through faith, we begin with the premise that organic life itself, including the cycles of birth, death, and decay, has some purpose in the universe, that through this cycling, some things of value revert to the universe that could not be had without this ongoing process. And while we are not able to know what these purposes might be, as this would be akin to understanding the mind of God, it is enough for us to take on faith that on this basic level, there must be some purpose and that for us is simply being part of organic life: Breathing, eating, growing, and dying fulfills a purpose.

On an intermediate level, 2L6–L7, the level that is typically called our mind, we as humans are capable of more than just our instinctive functions. We respond to the impressions we take in through our senses by forging relationships, learning skills, and becoming productive members of society. Further, by right living and the practice of certain forms of discipline, we can strengthen our hearts and minds, allowing a life of greater feeling and intentionality. But as much as we are part of an evolutionary process, we are also part of a devolutionary process, as when these energies flag, we become less of who we are. We become more fixed by habits, less open to experience, and less curious about the world in which we live. We become more like automatons with cold hearts and fixed minds. In the absence of an impulse of healing and sufficient mental and emotional energy, the seeds for heart diseases from frozen emotions and dementias from rigid thought patterns sprout and we end up dying by thirds, with the body being last to go.

But on the basis of faith, our premise is that the fruits of our hearts and minds—our relationships and our development—have purposes for the universe beyond our everyday existence. And though we can't know these purposes, our interior experience reveals at least one of them: that our thoughts, passions, and appetites not only outwardly affect those within our orbit but from a higher perspective, these also enable spirits to live through us, fulfilling their need, attraction, or wish to manifest through what is alive, with us being the means for this expression.

On the highest level, 3L, the level that is typically called our spirit, we reach what makes us uniquely human: We have the choice to not just respond automatically to the impressions we take in, but to reflect upon them and curate our experience as well. By so doing, we can choose how we expend our energies and can develop an opening to receiving higher energies from the world of spirit, including what the Bible calls the Holy Spirit, which for us would include the grace of healing.

3L is a great mystery because humans can function perfectly well without it—it is not an automatic part of our development but one that must be cultivated through appropriate means. And unlike the two prior levels that are intimately woven into the fabric of our physical bodies, here there is no material element but simply a refinement of the spiritual superstructure of harmonic resonance, so there is not an inevitable devolution. Something permanent may form—a soul—that can persist beyond the death of the body. Yet, healing may also have a part to play on this level as feelings of spiritual desolation and existential dread—the so-called dark night of the soul—can greatly benefit from appropriate forms of help.

Development of 3L, typically through faith-based or spiritual training, becomes the soul that curates our experience of the world and our manifestations in the world. Though we can't know why we have been given this capacity for self-awareness or why we have been given the possibility to reconfigure our machinery in ways that profoundly affect what flows through us, we find guidance on these questions in religious teachings. The Bible concerns itself with this question above all others. To paraphrase the Great Commandment, "Love God with all your heart, soul, mind, and strength and love your neighbor as yourself." God has given us free will and with it the ability to choose to live principally in the service of our default appetites, passions, and thoughts or, by recognizing our existence as his earthly agents and by diligent means, assist him in bringing his love into the world. In spiritual terms, we each stand at the confluence of two enormous rivers: the upward flow of the energy of life and the downward flow of the energy of grace, and by learning to harness these, we can bring a bit of heaven down to Earth for our own benefit and for the benefit of others.

For us in the healing professions, it is like the parable of the Good Samaritan. A lawyer asks Jesus how to define "one's neighbor." In the parable, a man is robbed and beaten and left on the side of the road and a Samaritan, coming upon this beaten man who was a stranger to him, does all in his power to help him recover, without any thought of himself.

If it has been put into our hearts to be part of a healing profession, we do all that we are able for the sake of our patients. We help "dry a tear in the eye of God." It is in this symbiosis between God's wish for his creation and our wish to assist him that we come to understand why we have been given the possibilities that fall to us as humans. But possibilities remain just that unless they are developed, and before we can understand that we must first understand this: What is healing?

CHAPTER 8

WHAT IS HEALING?

WE'VE GONE DEEP INTO the workings of consciousness and how it interfaces with life so that we may form an inclusive model of healing, taking into consideration several different systems of medicine and faith-based traditions. As far apart as these systems and traditions are from one another, our definition must identify what is common to all of them. So, before we get to a definition, it will help to apply our model to some examples that we have already covered and to some other real-life scenarios in order to gain some anchor points for this otherwise abstract subject.

At age six, Madeline is playing outside and her mother is watching her. In an instant, she falls and bruises her knee. She cries and runs to mommy, who gives her a hug and tells her that everything will be okay. Mommy cleans up the scrape, puts a bandage on it, kisses the knee, and Madeline, no longer crying, runs out again to play.

The mother addressed two separate issues: healing needed to begin both at the physical level of the bruise (2L1) and within the emotional level of Madeline's inner life (2L3–L5). At the physical level, the fabric of skin over her knee was torn. Bleeding began and a biological process of repair needed to begin. Let us focus on the moment that the breach occurred in the fabric of her cells.

The community of cells that form our surface are in constant communication with one another through a process called cell signaling, a phenomenon well understood by cell biologists. That is what happens on the material level. In our model, we describe a conscious connection within a community of cells occurring through the quality of resonance and how, through harmonic resonance, this level is embedded in the levels below and above it. Think of resonance as a kind of harmonic sound, like a church choir toning a long, harmonious chord, that alerts the cells that all is well. When there is a breach, this tone changes, and the choir needs a signal from a higher level to bring them back into resonance, such as a choirmaster providing a note on a pitch pipe. This is akin to the impulse of healing and it is possible in living systems because through harmonic resonance there is always oversight through a subsequent level above. In this case, 2L2, the level of complexity of organ systems, oversees 2L1, the level of complexity of cellular communities.

Now, let us assume that for whatever reason, Madeline's skin cells aren't getting the normally generated impulse to begin healing her bruise. In such an instance, that help can come from the outside, where, so to speak, a substitute choirmaster can sound the appropriate pitch and bring the choir back into resonance. This is how we must think about healing. While treatment is an intellectual thing, the impulse of healing is not thought-based. Every form of healing is a variation on this theme. The nature and complexity of the tone will change, and the nature and complexity of the choirmaster will change, but on every level an immaterial impulse from a higher level precedes a reharmonization process on a lower level. Healing then shares a similar dynamic with intuition, inspiration, and the revelatory states of grace where a higher level of consciousness sheds light and reharmonizes our understanding or our state.

In this example, young Madeline also became fearful and began to cry. Her mom gave her comfort and reassurance. In this instance, there was a similar bruise within Madeline's emotional center. With enough time, had she just been on her own, she would have stopped crying. But perhaps without this impulse of comfort and reassurance from her mother, a scar might have formed on her young, emotional center—thoughts like "play is dangerous" or "be afraid of sidewalks." But her mother served the purpose of choirmaster and sounded just the right tone to heal her daughter's emotional center, and all without a scar. Unlike therapy, which requires some intellectual understanding from the patient, the impulse of healing on this level itself is emotionally rather than intellectually based.

Now, Madeline is older and has had her first boyfriend, and sadly, it did not end well! Madeline is heartbroken and inconsolable! She feels grief in her heart, longing in her body, loneliness in her loss, and aloneness in her soul. For who else could ever understand how hard it is to have lost at love?

On each of these levels, healing will only come when Madeline is ready, and right now, words are of no comfort. But, in time, a tone will sound and that part of Madeline's being will resonate, "Oh. Yes . . . I remember now . . . that feeling of wholeness, that feeling of belonging, that feeling of joy in life." A parent, a friend, a relative, or a counselor—saying the right word at just the right time, or simply being present—these are the choirmasters who will help bring Madeline's soul, in all of its complexity, back into resonance. For this kind of injury, healing requires intuition (S5) in knowing just the right words, inspiration (S6) in knowing when to be silent and when to offer more, and the grace of healing itself (S7)—an atmosphere of compassion, love, acceptance, safety, peace, non-overbearingness, and the comfort of a nonjudgmental and impeccable moral presence.

But now, she craves aloneness. Where might she find it? There's an old stone church not far from her home, with soaring walls, stained glass panes, and vast reserves of quiet. She goes and sits in an empty pew at a time without a service. She cries and stops but lingers there and, without merit or plea, the spirit of grief ensnaring her heart is slackened by a higher force, a spirit of solace intended there, nesting in that space. Prayers without end have imbued this into the walls and the pews and the light. And there it dwells as a ring resides in a bell still yet to be rung. And sensing a chance to come alive and flow through a living heart, it quickens Madeline's spirit in perfect consolation.

Recall now the story of Grace Wiley, the herpetologist from the Zoo of Happiness. She was able to tame wild, poisonous snakes by her manner of being, her attention, and her patience, or, to state this more precisely, by her intent, the strength of her awareness, and her integrity to be in accord with the highest kind of love. If we can conceive of any living thing being in a state of fear, then bringing that being into a state of safety is healing on its most basic level: that of its instinctive energy. A snake in the wild harmonizes its own aroused state by attacking a target. But Grace Wiley transformed this fearful state by changing the atmosphere in the room so that fear had no place. She became choirmaster and set just the right tone at just the right time. And she was able to do this by positioning her awareness at a level of oversight above the snake's inner state. To do this, she had to be able to quiet her own inner states sufficiently so that she could fully and completely experience the snake's own world. And within this, she had to keep herself completely grounded in her own being so as not to be taken up by the snake's aggression. And within all of that, she had to create an atmosphere of calm and safety so enveloping within the room that, like iron filings drawn to a strong magnet, the snake was drawn into her calmness.

Finally, recall now the story of the miracle healing of Anne Theresa O'Neill, approaching death with no hope of cure. She was laid at the grave of the future saint Elizabeth Ann Seton and prayed for, only to make a complete recovery. Here we have a situation similar to Madeline gaining solace from the sacred space of the church, not for a broken heart but for a raging leukemia, and not from general prayers of solace but from specific prayers, focused and amplified through the lens of a sacred being. It seems that a characteristic of healing is that general intentions give general results and focused intentions give focused results, with the degrees of efficacy and specificity determined by what qualities can be brought into that moment. Here the choirmaster is God, and the mystery of spirit, the mystery of prayer, and the mystery of healing all come together. In Western medicine it is called a *spontaneous remission*, which is a catchall term for inexplicable healing. It is a term of convenience that any true scientist ought to take as a challenge for modeling a new hypothesis, even one that doesn't neatly fit into Western Materialism. But these cases sit like elephants in the middle of a room. Cures like what happened to Anne Theresa O'Neill beg for a larger model of healing than what Western medicine currently allows.

So, what is healing? It is the toning of a choirmaster, an impulse from a higher level that sounds the right tone at the right time to bring a lower level back into harmony. This is true on every level of life, from the level of a skinned knee to the level of a broken heart to the level of a grieving soul. And it is an impulse that may be self-generated or, if need be, it can come from the outside. When it is self-generated, it is just a common, everyday event of life, indeed, an event that makes life possible. But when this comes from the outside, an important point bears repeating.

When there is an illness, a Western medicine doctor will run tests to see what blood and urine values are off and will offer medicine to counter the outlying values, helping to bring the patient's biochemistry back into balance. A Chinese medicine doctor will assess an intricate reading of a patient's pulse and a reading of her tongue and then place acupuncture needles in precisely chosen points to rebalance her chi or life force. A doctor of Ayurvedic medicine will assess a patient's doshas, which are manifestations of her prana or life energy, and prescribe appropriate herbs and treatments to rebalance her. A homeopath will take a patient's history, develop a symptom picture that points to a specific remedy that resonates with those symptoms, and use it to rebalance her vital force.

Each of these modalities are like tools in a toolbox and each relies on an abstract third-person science or model of life, illness, and recovery. These treatment tools can be blind to the vast and intricate web of multilevel interconnections that comprise our own harmonic resonances. In naturally occurring healing, there is no abstraction and no intellectualization: It is an intuiting, an intending, or a praying from a higher level that brings a lower level back into harmony.

Now that we have covered the science, we can turn our attention to the kinds of practices that foster this kind of atmosphere. For simple things, a mother's kiss is all that is needed; for complex things, only the grace of God or the intervention of a saint can bring about a miracle. But for everything in between, there are those both inside and outside of the healing professions who—by a combination of effort, wish, and grace—have come to understand how to be of service in drying a tear in the eye of God. We will now explore practices that can assist those who wish to grow proficient in this art.

CHAPTER 9

THE REALM OF THE POSSIBLE

HAVING LAID OUT a theory of healing, we are now in a position to ask three practical questions. First, in day-to-day practice, what is possible? Second, given what is possible, by what means? And finally, how may one best prepare oneself to be effective?

If we view the two previous examples of Madeline and Anne Theresa O'Neill as being on opposite ends of a spectrum, then the scope of what is possible is quite wide as our definition of healing spans many levels. On one end, we have the common action of instinctive compassion, and on the other, we have the rare action of spiritual practices setting the stage for an extraordinary grace. Most situations are somewhere in the middle, between the common and the rare. Viewed from the outside, what might a patient experience?

On the simplest level, think of how Grace Wiley and the atmosphere she created was experienced by the snake. Each of us through our fourteen or fifteen levels of consciousness are infused and surrounded by a palpable atmosphere. Let's review some examples, some of which we first explored in chapter 6. If you have ever been in the presence of a world-famous individual, there is often an aura around him or her that we experience as charisma. If you have ever been around a hardened criminal or a truly violent person, you no doubt will feel something of the danger around them. Finally, if you have ever been around a truly holy person, there is a palpable feeling of holiness. These are all examples of the atmospheres that emanate from and surround each of us, and it is very much a matter of how we comport our lives that determines our own atmosphere. For Grace Wiley, the consistency of her intent, the strength of her awareness, and her integrity to be in accord with the highest kind of love created an atmosphere around her that was strong enough to fill a room and coherent enough with the spirit of snakes that they were tamed when in her presence.

For us, even beginners in this art ought to be able to create a palpable mood of calmness and safety within their immediate presence. On an intermediate level, even a casual but intentional touch ought to help regulate stress, decrease pain, and accelerate the healing process. If this were all that was possible, we could stop right here and simply call this good bedside manner. But these basic and intermediate levels merely set the stage for the diligent practitioner of this art. When a practitioner's efforts at the practices presented here begin to bear fruit, she first becomes open to intuitive and inspirational knowing regarding her patient, and with continued practice a coherent channel forms for revelatory states of grace including an atmosphere of healing. Intuition and inspiration can play major roles in patient care—imparting a sense of the scale or prominence of each sign and symptom, revealing layers of a patient's emotional connections with the suffering, and suggesting courses of care that may be a bit unconventional. These higher feelings are not the result of rational speculation on the one hand or fantasy on the other, but an understanding mediated by direct apprehension, what Thomas Aquinas described as being the nonrational, nondeductive way of knowing. Clearly, anyone with no more than a compassionate disposition will have some efficacy, but more, much more, is possible. This brings us to our second question: By what means?

So far, we have focused on the aspects of healing that activate a process. But there is another aspect to consider. Taking Madeline's skinned knee as an example, our scenario presupposes that Madeline is relatively healthy and possesses sufficient reserves of energy so that once directed, her cells can muster themselves to make repairs. But what if Madeline is deficient in energy? Can it, along with a choirmaster's toning, be supplied from the outside? The answer is, it depends.

Like healing in general, there are no guarantees; healing is not the same as curing and sometimes, particularly near the end of life, instinctive energy wanes as the higher energies of spirit begin their transition. In such a case, supplying instinctive energy may be inappropriate or impossible. But let us take a simpler case: Suppose Madeline has what a doctor of Chinese medicine would call chi deficiency. Then a practitioner of External Qigong could supply emitted chi to Madeline through finger contacts at specific acupuncture points or through other, noncontact means. The technique is based on a principle that we can store excessive amounts of our energies and, through various means, transfer some of that energy to others for therapeutic gain.

Returning to our analogy of the choirmaster, we see that what is needed is a kind of nonintellectual, superconscious impulse, something that we can intend, but we can never truly understand as it comes from a level above our rationality. But there is more to it than this. A good choirmaster loves her choristers and only wants to bring out the best in their individual voices so that the collective voice of the choir is the best that it can be. The choristers in turn love their choirmaster who, they feel, has only their best interests at heart. There is no ego and no politics. While the choristers' greatest talents are their voices, the choirmaster's greatest talents are her ears and her heart. She listens with respect, gentleness, and love, the same qualities that Grace Wiley used to tame wild snakes, and corrects the group with the pitch pipe and corrects individual choristers if she hears one who is out of key. So, in terms of one level having oversight of another level and serving as choirmaster, this relationship is a natural thing. But if help is going to come in from the outside, there needs to be this same kind of relationship between the practitioner and the patient. These are the conditions for restoring harmonic resonance from the outside. The injured level must accept the choirmaster, not out of coercion, but out of the same respect, gentleness, and love that must be forthcoming first from the practitioner. It is like the parable in the Gospel of John 10:27, "My sheep hear my voice. I know them, and they follow me." This is not to be taken as a need for a patient to worship a practitioner, but the need for a practitioner to create a condition, an atmosphere of healing, that opens the door for one who is injured to feel completely safe and taken care of.

So, for us to reach the highest levels of what is possible, we must stop losing our instinctive, emotional, and mental energies unnecessarily and store what we don't immediately require for our daily existence. Through appropriate means, we can use these energies to tame our appetites, passions, and thoughts, as well as to harmonize our instinctive, emotional, and mental energies so that we may become coherent with the higher spirits of intuition, inspiration, revelation, and the grace of healing itself. Finally, we may then be in a position to supply energy to our patients through various means.

In Chinese medicine there is a belief that chi, which approximates our instinctive energy, comes up from the earth and enters us through the kidney acupuncture meridians on the soles of each of our feet. It is likely that this can be understood both literally and figuratively because as living beings, our structure and our life do emerge from the earth in terms of the molecules of our bodies, the food that we eat, and the air that we breathe. All of these elements are from the earth. Eastern religions pinpoint the influx of the highest spirit, which approximates grace, entering us through the crown chakra at the top of our head, and Christianity speaks of the Holy Spirit descending into us from heaven, with no mention of any specific anatomic location. If we view these traditions as valid approximations of a truth gained through the science of interior experience, then we as humans stand at the confluence of two enormous rivers: a flow up from the earth and a flow down from heaven, and these come together in our center, in our heart, and we have the possibility to reconcile these for our own benefit and for the benefit of others if we can simply learn how.

So, to answer the second question: Given what is possible, by what means? We stand amid a great flux of energies, and these drive our lives with the barest need for our participation. But we are given a chance through our God-given consciousness to tend to our own machine and gain some control over the energies that flow through us and, through additional means, harness those flows toward therapeutic aims. In simple cases, all we need is a particular kind of compassion. In heroic cases, all we can offer is the highest degree to which we have developed our art. In this book, I am not suggesting that we strive to be saints and aim to work miracles. That is a different path. Yet, we can learn much from the saints in terms of how to become better instruments in the hands of God. For example, St. Teresa of Ávila in her book

The Interior Castle, written for the nuns of her Carmelite order, offered this distinction between prayers for self-perfection and prayers to be of service to others (see ICS Publications, second edition, 2020, of this book): "We should desire and engage in prayer not for our own enjoyment but for the sake of acquiring this strength which fits us for service." Many religious and spiritual traditions have devoted millennia to finding practices that aid in the perfection of the soul. Some of these are particularly useful in developing the capacity to create and maintain an atmosphere of healing.

So, in answer to our third question: How may one best prepare oneself to be effective? We now must explore a number of practices that aim to harmonize and strengthen the energies within us so that we may be of help in drying a tear in the eye of God.

CHAPTER 10

PRACTICES: INTRODUCTION

WE NOW OPEN A door to the prospect of bringing more to our patients than our competence and confidence. In the purely materialistic world of Western science, that is all there is. But if we are living in a layered world of spirit that is open to the ever-present potential for healing, then we have a higher obligation.

Let us consider the creation and maintenance of an atmosphere of healing to be the highest of the healing arts and set mastery of it as our aim. Some may argue that having the capacity to heal a particular person through touch, prayer, or other means ought to be considered the highest form of this art, but I would counter this argument in three ways. First, you have to be a good generalist before you can ever hope to be a good specialist. Second, one may have a strong bond with a particular person and through those means be able to bring about healing, but those may be ineffective with anyone else; recall, for example, the case of Madeline's mother. So, this would be less the practice of an art form than it would be a manifestation of personal love. Third, claiming to be a healer is an attitude fraught with arrogance and, as we shall learn, arrogance is the single most effective means by which to inhibit any impulse of healing.

As with any art form, some will be more talented than others, and some, with less talent and more diligence, will become more proficient than the innately talented. But healing is not a contest; comparing one's effectiveness to anyone else's is a form of arrogance that will work to the detriment of this aim. Also, healing is not a race; understanding the science and mastering its practices is a lifelong pursuit with the goal of always striving to be a better channel.

We can say just a few things about the grace of healing itself. It is the highest aspect of the Consciousness of Spirit that we are aspiring toward, and as we have discussed, there is a lengthy historic record, particularly within the Catholic Church, that humans can channel this grace to a greater or a lesser degree. This channeling is dependent on grace itself, over which we have no control, and on our ability to create and maintain a particular coherency. If we look to the historic record, those who have been effective at maintaining this coherency are those who have held a sacredness within themselves, manifesting to others in their presence as a feeling of the highest kinds of truth, goodness, and beauty. We refined this idea when in previous chapters we explored bringing our consciousness up to higher levels through the qualities of strength of awareness, intent, and integrity to be in accord with the highest kind of love, with obvious similarities between these qualities and those of sacredness. Further, we have explored how each of these qualities exist in us in fluctuating quantities, tied to our pools of mental energy, instinctive energy, and emotional energy, and how each of those three are, in turn, connected in overlapping groupings to the seven qualities of energy present in our seven 2L levels of consciousness. Finally, we have seen how the default exchanges between our life and the world of spirit tend to act as a drain on our energies, the same energies that we require to create and maintain a channel for grace.

In the following chapters, I will offer practices that are designed to build up and harmonize intent, strength of awareness, and integrity to be in accord with the highest kind of love, with the aim of creating and maintaining an atmosphere of healing. Unlike spiritual aspirants whose practices are exclusively interior in their quest for union with God, enlightenment, sainthood, and so on, our practices contain inner and outer components as our aim is not for development that holds only within a cloister, but for development that holds in the presence of patients. To make this point clearer, if you have ever done any kind of closed-eyed meditation and achieved a particular sense of presence, then you have likely experienced the moment of opening your eyes, observing your surroundings, and quickly losing that sense of presence. For our aim, we must so strengthen and harmonize our energies that we can maintain the quality of our presence even with our eyes open and in full interaction with those around us.

The practices that follow are to be considered in the same way that a pianist considers playing the scales. For the beginner, scales are about learning where the notes are and how to strike them. For the intermediary, they are about developing dexterity and speed. For the concert pianist, they are about keeping themselves aligned with their instrument so that as a pair, extraordinary feelings may be expressed. Like music, healing is an art form, and practice, in one form or another, is a lifelong pursuit.

CHAPTER 11

FIRST-ORDER PRACTICES: HARMONIZATION

UNLIKE SHAMANS WHOSE apprenticeships harmonize and strengthen their instinctive energies and open them to intuitive modes of knowing, those of us trained in Western medicine lack those particular refinements. Instead, our education focuses on improving our deductive modes of knowing through the refinement of our mental energies alone. After Galileo and the Council of Trent, Western medicine developed exclusively from rational thought, and this was a crucial departure from the folk remedies and superstitions of the Dark Ages. But for *healing*, we require what Thomas Aquinas described as "direct supernatural apprehension" (in *Aquinas's Shorter Summa*) and what we describe as an internal coherence sufficient for our alignment with higher orders of spirit. This has nothing to do with thoughts, thinking, or ideas.

We must begin by reconfiguring our thinking, emotional, and instinctive centers—2L1–L3, 2L3–L5, and 2L5–L7—so that they function harmoniously and as coequals rather than what we have as the birthright of our Western education: a thinking center that consumes us to the point that we are so identified with our thoughts that we have no perspective of them, but only immersion in them. Changing this can be accomplished through a combination of elevating the content of the S1, S2, and S3 linkages to be less accidental and more intentional and through cultivating our 3L level of consciousness from whence springs our conscience. 3L is the natural choirmaster of 2L and, given the chance, it can heal the disharmonies that obstruct our channels of grace.

Toward this end we will be using our attention to train our awareness, such that our awareness may flood all aspects of our being beyond its habitual focus solely within our thinking center. We do this by moving our awareness from its habitual perch in 2L5 and 2L6 up to 3L. Once 3L establishes parity among the centers, Second-Order practices can be added to the First-Order ones presented here. Second-Order practices, presented beginning in chapter 12, aim to increase the energies inherent in each of the 2L levels, which, when they combine, yield our instinctive, emotional, and mental energies. These energies in turn, when refined through internal coherence, give rise to what we require for creating and maintaining an atmosphere of healing: our intent, the strength of our awareness, and integrity to be in accord with the highest kind of love.

It would be counterproductive to increase these energies, particularly the emotional energies, prior to the harmonization of our centers for the same reason that it is dangerous to build up the strength of a wild horse before it can be tamed. In fact, First-Order practices steer clear of engaging at all in the S2 linkages to our emotional energies and aim simply to elevate the content of our links with S1 and S3. We have to be particularly careful with the development of compassion. I will have more to say about this in a moment when I clarify the concept of patience, and then more specifically about compassion, at the end of this chapter.

Once the centers are harmonized, having additional energy increases the strength of the atmosphere around us and the strength of the atmosphere we imbue into the spaces we occupy. Yet, none of that guarantees that this now stronger and more harmonized atmosphere will be one of healing unless we are consistent in holding fast to our aim. For example, you may believe yourself to be familiar with some of the practices that follow. One of them shares traits with what is popularly known as Mindfulness-Based Stress Reduction (MBSR). And while there are similarities, our aim in that case is not stress reduction but elevating the level of intentionality in the link between 2L1–L3 and S1, as that is a rung on the ladder toward an atmosphere of healing. As well, in chapter 12, I will be recommending practices that may be available at local gyms, dance studios, or dojos. And while you may take class and train just like everyone else, always keep your aim in mind: You are pursuing these practices not for the disciplines themselves but for how they will help you reach your aim. In this sense, your aim is your prayer, and as St. Paul famously said in 1 Thessalonians 5:17, "Pray without ceasing."

One last bit of advice: Always and in everything, cultivate an elevation in your threshold for frustration. Inevitably, these practices will demonstrate to you just how far you are from your aim, and the work to get there can be tedious and full of setbacks. So, make it a point to grow in patience every day, but a very particular kind of patience.

Among the Second-Order practices that we will cover in the next chapter will be ones for strengthening emotional energy, and a part of that will involve having patience with others. But it is impossible to be patient with others in any genuine way if one doesn't have a particular kind of patience with one's self. At this point, I want to make a clear distinction: It is common in our culture for individuals to talk about giving themselves "me time" and elevating their efforts to take care of themselves or pamper themselves, and this can be construed as having a kind of patience with oneself. This kind of patience can easily extend to include excusing all kinds of self-serving appetites, passions, and indulgences, which, in the context of our subject, are counterproductive.

I am not suggesting that anyone live in austerity. For these practices to work, it is important to have, paraphrasing the Christian mystic George Gurdjieff, "everything satisfying and really necessary for your health and well-being." But justifying excesses through the lens of patience distorts the sense in which I am using this term. I am advocating that you be patient not with the weaknesses of your personality—for those you must be relentless! But I am advocating that you be patient with the formation of your essence: your soul. Patience in this regard will play an ever-enlarging role in your capacity for compassion and will greatly help you with your aim.

Strengthening Attention, Awareness, and Intent

This exercise is to be practiced privately or, if in a group setting, only with others who are also practicing and in which case someone designated as the leader can speak in the first person and verbalize the directions while performing the steps. In the beginning, practice should last no more than twenty minutes as this will mark the upper limit of your strength. We will be using the spotlight of attention to tame the thought stream by focusing on increasingly subtle sensations. Over time the earlier steps will require less of the spotlight of attention as they will function more through the floodlight of awareness. In this way once our awareness becomes educated to a particular field of focus, our attention becomes free to concentrate on subsequent steps. Eventually this entire practice will fall into the realm of awareness and our attention will be free for working with patients in a very new way.

If during any part of this exercise you discover that a thought stream has taken your attention, just acknowledge this without judgment or emotion, and return to the last place that you can remember before your attention was taken from you. A key to these First-Order exercises is that except where you are given specific instructions to use your observations to make changes in your state as, for example, where you are told to look for areas of tension and release them, you are in all other circumstances to simply observe your experiences dispassionately, without mental, emotional, or instinctive comment or urge to make a change. We are using these practices in part to resonate with 3L, a level above our default states or self-talk, vanity, pride, beliefs in self-control, and so on. Consciousness centered in 3L is thought-free and open to the higher-order spirits of grace, which give us access to the sacred within our everyday experience. Remember, consciousness is not continuous like a ramp but proceeds like rungs on a ladder, similar to how electrons within an atom jump or fall into higher or lower orbits, depending on the quality and quantity of energy available. We require the energy we save by taming our thoughts, appetites, and passions to jump our 2L-centered experience up to 3L.

As you make progress you will strengthen your attention, your awareness, and your intent. Like muscles that have been exercised, you will have an increased capacity to stay in this practice longer. In fact, advanced practitioners will need about forty minutes to complete all the steps. In the beginning when awareness and intent are weak and disorganized, it will be enough simply to try to get all the way through step one. In fact, it may take a week or more of daily practice simply to master step one. Once step one proceeds smoothly, you can begin step two. This process continues until you can get through all seven steps. Whenever practicing this exercise, always start with step one and proceed sequentially through as many steps as you have the capacity to complete. It is like learning a sacred dance, and you need to take all the time you need to learn each step thoroughly before moving on to learn the next step, as the skills for mastering one step help with the next step.

In a quiet room, without draft or bright light and where you won't be distracted or interrupted, sit on a stool or in a chair that will allow you to sit up straight, without leaning on a chairback. With shoes off, rest the soles of your feet flat on the ground, place your hands palms up, back of one hand resting on the palm of the other, and rest them in your lap and close your eyes.

STEP ONE: SENSING ALIGNMENT IN GRAVITY

Notice how the force of gravity affects your body. Focus your attention on sensing where your weight falls. It will be mostly on your seat, but some of it will also be on the soles of your feet. Depending on your posture, you may feel tension if you are not properly aligned. For example, if you tend to sit with your head positioned in front of the plane of your body, you will sense tension on the back of your neck and in your shoulders and upper back. If you tend to sit slouched forward, then you will sense tension in your middle and upper back, and if you tend to overly tilt your pelvis forward, then you will feel tension in your lower back. Make corrections in your body within the field of gravity to minimize all postural tensions, including evenly distributing your weight on your seat. Aim to sit as if a string was connected to the top of your head and was holding it upright like a marionette puppet, with your arms and legs completely relaxed. Aim so that the only places where you have any sensation of your weight falling are your seat, the soles of your feet, and the weight of your hands resting against your lap.

STEP TWO: SENSING LIFE

Slowly and systematically use your attention to walk throughout your body as a night watchman with a flashlight might do within a building, "separating light from darkness," as is said in Genesis 1:4. In this case, you are looking for habitual muscle tensions that are not needed for supporting posture. When you find these, then with attention and curiosity, examine them for their size, shape, and quality of sensation and sit with them as if they were a stranger that you were trying to get to know. Focus all of your attention and hold it on these tension spots until they naturally release on their own and then continue your patrol. Your aim is to reduce, to the greatest extent possible, the energy that your body burns through when it holds unnecessary muscle tensions. Additionally, you want to be able to sense the fine vibration-like sensation of life that is ever present but hidden under the more prominent sensations of muscular tension.

Starting with your right leg at the top of the thigh, slowly walk your attention down through your muscles to the knee, then to the calf muscles, the ankle, the foot, and the toes. Repeat this for your left leg, left arm, right arm, then scan from the top of your head, stopping at your face, being sure that all of your muscles of facial expression are relaxed, especially those around the eyes, between the eyebrows, around the mouth, and that the jaw is not clenching and the tongue is at rest. Then continue down your neck, shoulders, and chest, to your solar plexus, gut, and ending at a point on the surface of your belly that lies about two inches below your navel. This point is your center of gravity and what Chinese medicine refers to as the *Tan Tien* or energy center. Concentrate your attention on the sensation of this center point and then let your awareness enlarge to encompass the entirety of this sensation of fine vibration throughout your body. With awareness of this whole, guide your attention to any spot or spots where there may still be traces of tension and attend to them until the tension releases on its own. Finally, sit in the awareness of your whole body as an upright, conscious, living object with a silent mind and whose only movement comes in your breathing.

STEP THREE: SENSING BREATH

Without altering its natural rhythm, follow the sensation of your breath. Begin with the sensation of the air, like the tide, entering and leaving your nose, noticing the brief pauses when the airflow changes direction. When you sense that your entire attention is well concentrated on the sensation around your nose, move your attention to your abdomen and follow the sensation of it expanding outward as you inhale and deflating as you exhale. When you sense that your entire attention is well concentrated on this sensation, move your attention into your chest. Sense your rib cage expanding and contracting as your lungs fill and empty, and on a more subtle level, sense the enlivening force that enters you with each inhalation. Notice that when you inhale you create a mild vacuum within your whole body, with your chest being the most noticeable place. Ninety-nine percent of our oxygen intake is through our lungs, but 1 percent comes in through our skin. This is most noticeable on the dorsal surfaces of the forearms and the backs of the hands. When you exhale you create a mild pressure wave throughout your body, with your chest being the most noticeable place. The 1 percent that leaves us through our skin is most noticeable on the ventral surfaces of our forearms and on the palmar surfaces of our hands. Focus now on this subtle, 1 percent respiration with your attention on the dorsum of your forearms and hands as you inhale and on the ventral surfaces of your forearms and the palmar surfaces of your hands as you exhale. Repeat until your entire attention is well concentrated on this sensation.

STEP FOUR: SENSING HEARTBEAT

Place your attention on the sensation of your heart beating; focus entirely on the sensation of its steady, regular pulsation in your chest. You will inevitably lose track of this sensation due to an intrusive thought stream or simply due to the strength of your attention becoming less than this subtle pulsation. When this happens, simply acknowledge this occurrence without judgment or emotion, and return your attention to the sensation of your heart beating. Repeat until your entire attention is so well concentrated on this sensation that you can easily follow it without losing your focus.

STEP FIVE: SENSING PULSE IN THE HANDS

Next, make a small adjustment in your hand postures so that instead of nesting with the palms up, the palms now face each other and the fingertips each come lightly into contact with the corresponding finger. Arrange your hands this way, supported by your lap, and adjust so that the pressure felt at each of the five points of contact feels equal to you. Now, briefly refocus your attention on your heartbeat in your chest and sense the pressure wave that begins at the heart and propagates down both arms and continues into your palms and into your fingertips. Stay with the sensation of this entire pressure wave from heart to fingertips for ten beats; if the strength of your attention becomes less than this sensation and you lose it, acknowledge the occurrence without judgment or emotion and begin again at the sensation of your heart beating in your chest. Once you can prolong your awareness from heart to fingertips for ten beats, then place all of your attention on the five points of contact between your left and right fingers. You will notice a slight sense of ballooning of the tips of each finger at the moment the pressure wave arrives. Concentrate all of your attention on this rhythmic ballooning as your fingertips briefly press tighter into one another owing to their temporarily enlarged volumes. Repeat until your entire attention is so well concentrated on this sensation that you can easily follow it without losing your focus.

STEP SIX: SENSING EXTERNAL CHI

Now, adjust your hand postures so that instead of them facing each other with fingertips touching, they now rest, palm up on their respective thighs, and focus your attention on the sensation in your hands of the rhythmic beating of your heart. Notice the warmth growing in your palms and fingers with each and every beat. Place your awareness on this growing "ball of warmth," and in a matter not unlike blowing up a balloon, intend, with the sensation of each beat of your heart and each exhaled breath, that this ball inflates bigger and bigger. Do not in any way alter your breathing pattern and don't purse your lips, and so on. Nothing should "show" as this exercise is entirely internal. Be careful not to speculate or imagine this sensation, but rather, you are sensing an expanding sensation of warmth. First, sense the ball as just sitting across both palms. Next, sense the warmth of the ball against your belly, about two inches below your navel. Next, sense it as encompassing your solar plexus as high as the lower border of your rib cage. Next, sense it as encompassing your chest as high as your clavicles, including your heart and lungs. Next, sense it up as high as your lower jaw and lower lip. Next, sense it as high as your eyebrows. Finally, sense it enveloping your whole body with its topmost surface reaching a few inches above the crown of your head.

STEP SEVEN: SENSING "JACOB'S LADDER"

Finally, in the same manner as you were sensing in step six, now aim to sense something even finer. Place your attention in your heartbeat and follow the pulse wave up to a point at the very top of your head and from that point sense the space just above it. Here, you will not be sensing a ball of warmth but a column of vibration that has a fainter, finer quality than the sensation of life in step two. Hold your attention on the sensation of this column that begins in your heart and ends in the space just above the crown of your head.

▪ ▪ ▪

These First-Order practices create a stable foundation from which your atmosphere of healing will arise. As we end this chapter, let us briefly explore the nature of this important stability. It is common for our awareness to be a bystander to all of our default exchanges, such that we are so engrossed in what is in front of us that we lose all sense of ourselves. A deep conversation, a dramatic novel or movie, or a video game can so engross us that at the end of our reverie we exclaim, "I don't know where the time went!" In fact, the central feature of all of the default exchanges that occur between S1–S3 and the lower, middle, and upper levels of 2L is that we are consumed by what we experience. Thoughts, passions, and appetites run through us and consume some of our energy. Mostly, we are completely unaware of what happened. Only in retrospect do we realize that we have little memory of these moments as we were not really "there" in them; rather, they just happened to us without need of our presence.

Now consider the more real and dramatic experience of taking care of a patient. It is easy to get consumed in this very real drama, and there are some who say that this shows empathy and caring—that a practitioner "has heart" and feels bad for the suffering in front of them. In truth, this sentiment prevents higher-order S4–S7 exchanges because for those to be possible, we must elevate ourselves out of our default alignments. We must strive for a higher order of consciousness, 3L, so that we are not consumed but can pick and choose where to expend our energies. And the single most effective way to train one's being not to be consumed by thoughts, passions, and appetites that are just passing through is by developing the ability to instantly switch from being present to one's thoughts to being present to one's body.

Our body is our anchor here on Earth and our awareness of it, its sensations, its rhythms, and its energies immediately anchor us to the here and now. Body awareness does not involve thought, and it does not involve speculation, memory, fantasy, or anticipation; it is just here and just now. When the woman with the hemorrhage was healed by touching Jesus's garment, it was his presence that did it. He was in the moment; he was not consumed by the pressing in of the crowds around him. What we can learn from the saints is that they have a presence that is stable, and from this foundation they are then able to be a channel for grace.

It is what I call "compassion without sympathy," and while we have yet to address the development of compassion, I assume that if you have gotten this far in this book, you already have a sense of compassion toward others, but hopefully not too much. Compassion developed at the level of 2L4 is inevitably stunted in a way that is largely unrecognized in our culture and, sadly, it is the most common form of compassion that we see. This deformity of growth stems from how what should be a manifestation of a higher order, of 3L, is limited when it develops solely from 2L, as from there it can be nothing more than a sentimental feeling that is limited to a particular individual at a particular time. It is a kind of love that is beautiful in a child, but in growing up and in striving to be a vessel for healing, we must develop a higher love and a higher compassion. It is the difference between asking oneself, "How compassionate can I be?" to being in a state where the question becomes "How much compassion can flow through me?" True compassion is impersonal, a product of what Thomas Merton (in *The Seven Storey Mountain*, 1998 edition) referred to as "God's infinitely disinterested love," a love that expects nothing in return, what I call love without possession.

But at this point we must make an important distinction. In our culture where so much emphasis is placed on our thinking center, it would be easy to mistake the idea of compassion without sympathy as being a way to stand apart from the suffering of another and to somehow intellectualize it and so not to be touched by it. This is not correct. Compassion comes from the heart, not from the mind, and as such true compassion opens the door to shouldering some of the pain being felt by another, as is written in Galatians 6:2—to "bear one another's burdens." We help another when we are present with them and, to the extent that we can feel their pain, we can help alleviate suffering. But by being grounded, we don't get taken by that suffering so that we can actually be effective. It is like the instructions given on an airplane for dealing with an emergency: Put the oxygen mask on yourself before you put it on your child, otherwise you may pass out before you can help anyone else.

In terms of developing compassion along the right lines, consider this analogy: When an English driver comes to America, the instinct to drive on the left must be unlearned and a new instinct must form in order to feel comfortable driving on the right. It is more difficult for him to alter his habitual instinct than it is for a sixteen-year-old with a learner's permit to learn from the beginning to drive on the right. In the same way, someone whose compassion fully develops in 2L4 will have a lot of unlearning to do if they are to re-form compassion under the influence of 3L. So, better to start with just a seed of compassion and then cultivate it from 3L, where it can develop free from deformity.

Let these First-Order practices serve not only to strengthen your attention, your awareness, and your intent, but also to give you a sense of your body as an anchor in the present moment. In this way you can instantly switch your awareness from its more habitual locus in your thought stream so that you can be compassionate without being consumed in your patient's suffering. This is compassion without sympathy, and possessing this quality is the first sign that the center of our awareness, our "I," is within 3L, at least for brief periods of time. In order for us to stabilize our presence within 3L, we require additional energy. And for that, Second-Order practices are called for.

CHAPTER 12

SECOND-ORDER PRACTICES: CONTINENCE

WITH THE STEPS we've taken toward harmonizing our thinking and instinctive centers, it's now important to begin the difficult task of taming our passions by increasing the energies of each of the 2L levels that feed our centers. Second-Order practices share some characteristics with First-Order practices in that there are some things to do on your own that do not require the presence of others. These practices are not necessarily meditative but are more like taking a particular kind of internal inventory. But, in addition, Second-Order practices also include elements where you may need a partner, a teacher, a group, or a class.

It is a matter of common experience that each of our centers has an independent reservoir of energy. For example, we can exhaust ourselves physically yet have plenty of focus to think, or we can exhaust ourselves emotionally and still have energy for physical work. Here, we are introducing the concept that it is not just the energies of our three centers that are unique, but that the energies of each of the 2L levels that feed those centers have their own character and their own reservoir. These combine outwardly into the groupings of threes that we have already discussed, and they form the thinking, feeling, and instinctive energies. They combine inwardly in ways that we have not yet discussed, forming links that have been the subject of esoteric traditions of the East and of the West for thousands of years.

For example, in the pre-Christian era, schools of alchemy that began in the ancient worlds of Egypt, Greece, China, and Persia had a stated goal of finding a method of turning base metals into gold. But alchemy was a practice with science and spirit firmly united. The outer metallurgical goal mirrored an inner goal of finding a method of transforming the lower energies of the body into the higher energies needed to perfect the soul. Also, the Hindu practices of Kundalini and Tantric yoga aim to channel the 2L1 energy that they locate at the base of the spine and have it rise, merge, and become refined with the energies 2L2–2L7. As well, celibacy within religious and spiritual communities has everything to do with transmuting the 2L2 energy into the finer energies needed for what is referred to as *infused contemplation*, the interior practice of preparing a channel through which the graces of God may flow.

Our purposes are consonant with all of these. Our aim is to create a persistent and robust channel suitable for the grace of healing to flow through. For this we must stop losing energy by accidental means from each of our 2L levels so that they accumulate to the point where excesses overflow and supplement the reservoirs they are connected to. But there is more to this than just preventing the loss of energy. For a channel to open for grace, each 2L reservoir must contain energy that has been harmonized with the energies of other 2L levels through what we have termed internal coherence. An analogy for this is to imagine each reservoir to be capable of circulating its energy in such a way that a channel opens up in its center, in the same way as an eye of a hurricane opens up in its center when the storm circulation is sufficiently organized.

When each of these channels is configured in this way, a clear channel forms that grace can flow through. Here, our model closely follows the Buddhist and Hindu anatomical structure of the major chakras, with the coarsest energy of 2L1 being located at the base of the spine and having excess energy overflow up to 2L2 at the location of the second chakra, and so on up to 2L7 at the crown of the head. It is worth noting that the functions of the major chakras given in chapter 6 can also be found in a modern-day equivalent: the hierarchy of needs as elaborated in the 1940s by the developmental psychologist Abraham Maslow. As such, much of the work in this chapter will involve areas of focus that are frequent targets of psychological counseling, although our focus will remain on the narrower subject of addressing energetic loss.

Here, it is also useful to consider an analogy from the world of locksmithing. There is a type of combination lock known as a cable lock that is commonly used for locking up bicycles. The lock consists of a cylinder whose surface is made up of four or five rotating rings, the edges of which are marked with the numbers zero to nine. When these rings are dialed into the combination of the lock, a clear channel is created and the cable-end piece can be cleanly inserted into the cylinder in order to lock up the bike, but while the numbers are jumbled relative to this combination, the channel is obstructed by one or more of the rings.

Now consider this: Within our energetic body the seven major chakras are akin to the rings of a cable lock, and mostly they are jumbled. If one happens to be open, others will be closed so that there is no clear channel. But if we find the right combination, we can open each chakra and by this means create a channel for the grace of healing to flow through us.

But chakras are not like numbered rings. For each of them to open, three criteria must be met. First, a sufficient amount of the energy unique to that chakra's 2L level must be present. As we saw in the example of my awareness during that professional lecture, the higher up 2L we go, the less of these energies we have. Second, the energy on each level must not be inadvertently lost due to leakage, as can happen in a way not unlike how milk in a full saucer can spill at its edge if the saucer is not properly balanced. Third, unlike the mechanical rings on a cable lock that remain open once the combination has been dialed in, each chakra requires a constant presence of harmonized energy in order to remain open, like a chain of little hurricanes each with an opened eye.

In the normal course of living, assuming adequate nutrition, sleep, daylight, and so on and in concert with the benefits accruing from the First-Order practices, each of the 2L levels ought to be getting sufficient energy for its own functioning. It is generally then not a matter of creating additional energy in any of those levels but of preventing the unintentional energetic losses that result from our default inner states. For this reason, the practices to follow are described in terms of developing *continence* in each of the 2L levels. Later, in the chapter on Third-Order practices, we will concentrate on *directing* the flow of these energies, something possible once we have stored sufficient quantities and harmonized the relations among them.

Second-Order practice needs vary from person to person because each of us contains different configurations of energetic leaks. For more on this topic, I point the reader to the first book of this trilogy, *The Charm Carver*, and the chapter entitled "Inner Wishes." It is because of this variation, person to person, that spiritual guides are so very helpful in directing our efforts to the practices that are essential for *us*. This book can only be a general guide, so what follows are practices that are specific to each 2L level. And while I recommend everyone spend a bit of time and attention on each of them, it is common that one of these seven levels comprises a primary leak, another a secondary leak, and a third a tertiary leak. These are often hard to spot in oneself but embarrassingly easy to spot in someone else! Again, a trusted spiritual guide can be enormously helpful in steering one's efforts to the most important place. In time, you will discover your own challenges with one or more of these levels and they will become lifetime practices toward ever greater perfection. All art forms work like this and healing is no different.

A hallmark of how 2L levels function when subject to default exchanges is that they lack all nuance and instead behave like switches that only exist in one of two extreme positions. It is only when we bring intentionality or conscience into our 2L coherences that connect life and spirit that these levels are capable of functioning with the flexibility present in all higher states of consciousness. So, preventing energetic losses in each of our levels involves finding ways to exist in the middle, between these two energetic extremes, a concept that happens to be central to the Chinese philosophy of Taoism. This will become clear once we get started.

CHAPTER 13

2L1 CONTINENCE: PRIMAL LIFE ENERGY

IN 2L1 LIES OUR primal life energy, which approximates chi in Chinese medicine. We lose 2L1 energy as a result of one of two opposite extremes: There will be either a craving of attention out of fear that one will not be seen and accepted, or else there will be some form of hiding out of fear that one is in danger. These two attitudes can be overt or subtle, and they may comprise a central or a peripheral role in one's personality. For our purposes, we assume that one's basic needs for food, clothing, shelter, and so forth are sufficient, so that for us 2L1 issues are a matter of one's life habits that result from one's personal history. These can manifest in obesity versus anorexia, hoarding versus asceticism, overbearingness versus timidity, and so on. It is not within our scope to delve into psychological approaches for addressing these imbalances. Our focus remains on practices for reducing the amount of 2L1 energy lost. These behaviors tend to become less prominent as 2L1 gains continence.

The practice attitude to assume is similar to that of the night watchman with the flashlight, given in the First-Order practices: When you find yourself in a position to observe one or the other end of this dichotomy in your own behavior, do not try to change it, but study it as if it were a stranger you are trying to get to know. Because we are dealing with something more complex than muscle tension, the quality of our attention and the strength of our intent must rise. It will not be enough simply to be attentive and curious. Now, in addition, it is necessary to observe these behaviors using the same qualities that Grace Wiley exhibited when taming a wild snake: respect, gentleness, and love. When you focus in this way, the source of this drain will weaken. The spirits that feed on 2L1 energy live through each of us. They are strengthened through fear and they are weakened by being recognized and being known. The spotlight of this quality of attention—attentive, curious, respectful, gentle, and loving—disperses spirits as light disperses a shadow. Be aware that holding this quality of attention is also a practice in self-directed compassion—*real* compassion, not tied to sympathy or need. It is only through educating our being in this way that we become capable of directing this same, clean compassion outwardly, through an atmosphere of healing.

Throughout these Second-Order practices we will be returning again and again to using this quality of attention, which is our conscience from 3L, to act as choirmaster and heal each of these levels. Simply through its focus, the energetic leaks subside and the accumulated energies become more and more harmonized and open to grace.

But make no mistake, while dispersing muscle tension through attentiveness and intent is a straightforward task, we are now beginning to address energetic leaks engrained through our appetites and passions, and these will not give up without a struggle. As we move up the 2L hierarchy, the forces of spiritual inertia, the spirits that through accidental coherences have established themselves firmly within our lives, will make this work increasingly difficult. When facing this conflict, always keep your aim in your heart and in your mind. Ultimately, the intention of your aim must eclipse the default state on each of your levels and the strength gained through every 2L continence will fuel your progress.

Further practices for 2L1 center on developing an abiding sense of the immediacy, corporeality, and groundedness of the physical body regardless of if you are lying down, sitting, standing, or moving about. The first practice is one to be done in public, but alone, without others' awareness of your practice. Beyond this you will find suggestions for additional practices that will help you in this regard. The list of these others is not exhaustive, and the reader is encouraged to use these suggestions or to find similar practices that may be more locally available.

But first, a few points about the need for and the benefit of keeping these public practices strictly to yourself. Although you will be learning various things from a teacher and you may be in a class-like setting, it will be important that you keep your inner aim strictly to yourself or share it only with others who have the same aim as you. There is a dispersal of one's force at the 2L5 level, of the very energies that we are trying to accumulate, that comes with excessive talk and excessive sharing. In addition, there is an easy shift from earnestness to pride and then to arrogance, which defeats our entire purpose in pursuing these practices. Finally, as I indicated earlier, your aim is your prayer, and as Jesus famously said (Matthew 6:5–6), "Whenever you pray, do not be like the hypocrites; for they love to stand and pray in the synagogues and at the street corners, so that they may be seen by others. Truly I tell you, they have received their reward. But whenever you pray, go into your room and shut the door and pray to your Father who is in secret; and your Father who sees in secret will reward you."

Pedestal Stance

I first presented this practice in the second book of this trilogy, *Letters to a Young Healer*, in the chapter entitled "On Vitality." It is best accomplished when you are standing in a crowd as may happen when you are waiting in a line. First, stand in a way that is comfortable for you, with a posture that will enable you to stand in that same position for an extended period of time without shifting your weight or adjusting your stance. Now imagine that the ground that each foot is standing on becomes elevated by one inch with nothing else changing. Now imagine that these one-inch pedestals rise up in the same manner that a car does when it is put up on a lift in a repair shop. In your mind, you are standing on these same footfalls, but you are now six feet off the ground. Finally, imagine that this lift continues upward and you are now one hundred feet off the ground. Your footfalls are exactly the same, and you are not balancing on a tightrope, but your feeling of safety from falling is remarkably different as the risk of falling from 100 feet is very different from the risk of falling when you are standing on the ground. Use this exercise to perfect your stance such that you can sense your weight down in the soles of your very relaxed feet and your entire body is held in good alignment.

Tai Chi Chuan

Many martial arts practices and yoga practices will give serious students a heightened sense of their relationship to gravity and a greater sense of their body. As well, ballet training and learning the art of fencing will largely accomplish the same thing. But for the specifics that we are looking for, no practice is more appropriate, more helpful, and more consonant with our aim than is Tai Chi Chuan and its related practices of Qigong and Tuishou, also known as "Push Hands."

Despite the fact that there are online courses and DVDs that can teach you the choreography, there is an extraordinary amount of nuance to this practice that requires, at least in the beginning, a well-qualified teacher, and there is much to learn from observing others struggling to learn the same thing as you.

Tai Chi teaches groundedness, balance, and movement, and it directly teaches how to store and channel 2L1 energy. The External Chi exercise from the First-Order practices is taken from Tai Chi and Qigong practices. Tuishou best falls under the category of a Third-Order practice that we will deal with in a later chapter, but we will introduce it here. Push Hands is a two-person practice that, at minimum, serves as a check on the quality of your Tai Chi practice by challenging you to maintain your balance when challenged from the outside. As mentioned before, one of the chief reasons for burnout among health-care professionals is that they can get so caught up in the suffering of patients that they lose the sense of their own groundedness and lose their energy to them. Most of this is an issue to be dealt with when we reach practices for 2L4, but developing what in Tai Chi is called "a strong root" serves as the foundation needed for a more stable 2L4.

VO_2 Max

In the same way as the accidental attunements of 2L1 tend toward two extremes, resulting in a loss of this energy, the tempo of 2L1 energies also tend to be restricted to just two extremes: either the tempo of sleep or the tempo of our default level of wakefulness.

In order to not lose so much 2L1 energy, it is necessary to force a new, third tempo on the body, one that requires a strong intention to achieve. This new tempo is best reached through some type of vigorous physical exercise such as running, playing an active sport such as tennis at a challenging pace, or anything similar. The expression "VO_2 Max" refers to the maximum volume of oxygen that a body can burn in any given unit of time. There are countless health benefits to this kind of exercise, but our purpose here is simply to intentionally drive the metabolism into a new, non-habitual tempo that will stretch the repertoire of 2L1. As such, there is no strict time requirement within this practice; even a regular practice of just one minute of full-out running or climbing stairs as part of a regular schedule of physical fitness will accomplish what you need from it.

CHAPTER 14

2L2 CONTINENCE: THE ENERGY OF CREATION

2L2 SERVES AS THE reservoir for our sexual energy, known as *Jing* in Chinese medicine, a fuel for all of our creations be they biological, artistic, emotional, intellectual, or spiritual. As such, 2L2 contains architectural features that are unique among all of the 2L levels. Each other level, while lacking internal coherence, only connects internally to the levels directly adjacent to it, forming a chain from 2L1 to 2L7. Yet from the outset 2L2 has direct anastomoses to each of the other levels, allowing it to fuel or drain our entire energetic system.

There are three ramifications to this. First, from a strictly "survival of the species" point of view, these connections assure that as long as there is at least some energy somewhere, there will always be energy to procreate a new generation. Second, along these same pathways, sexual energy can flow *from* 2L2 into any of the other levels. This is beneficial because if we can store the energy of 2L2, we can learn to use it to bolster any of our other levels, including using it, for example, to fuel our jump from 2L7 up to 3L, as is the aim of the celibate contemplative orders. In each of these two examples, there is a request from some level to receive help from 2L2.

But there is a third ramification to this architecture, where 2L2 is not requested to flow to any of the other levels, but instead through one of two opposite extremes it is pushed out of the 2L2 reservoir into other levels, whether they want it or not. This is the default configuration that we commonly find in our culture, and this is how, like a saucer of milk tipped this way or that, 2L2 energy is spilled. One of these extremes is through a kind of inhibition of shame, where 2L2 energy is put into the service of hypersexualized thoughts, feelings, and actions. These manifest, for example, through misogyny, pornography, or any of the myriad forms of what might be called sexual adventurism. In the other extreme, the energy is lost through a kind of hypertrophy of shame, where those who have suffered from some form of abuse purge their 2L2 energy through all available means, resulting, for example, in elaborate fantasies, gratuitous emotional displays, or the catastrophizing of future events. Put simply, 2L2 energy is lost when shame in one extreme or the other is subverted into an unconscious habit rather than serving as a prompt for conscience.

These two energetic extremes can be overt or subtle, and they may comprise a central or a peripheral role in one's personality.

Because of 2L2's multichannel anastomosis, any drain from 2L2 through either extreme triggers a drain from other energetic levels, the most common being from 2L3, the source of one's will, and from 2L4, the source of one's emotions. So, preventing loss of 2L2 energy is foundational to our Second-Order practices. Continence here creates conditions for virtue and trust to become part of our atmosphere. For this we must take up practices that will overrule the habits present at either extreme of 2L2 energy loss and yield to us the freedom to use this energy in more intentional ways.

But habits are hard to break, because some kind of satisfaction results from them. So, breaking a habit relies on convincing some inner aspect of ourselves that there is a greater reward than that provided by the habit itself. We did not have this issue in 2L1, because there is no inherent pleasure that comes from excessive muscle tension. Those are habits of alignment, and though there are spirits that are drawn into and perpetuate those postures, it is easier to disperse them as they lack the leverage that comes when spirits are anchored through a hunger or a passion. But with a level such as 2L2, that is so intimately connected with pleasure, we face a real struggle. So, how do we approach this?

We must come back to our aim. If it is our wish to master the art of creating and maintaining an atmosphere of healing, then it is this aim that gives us the leverage, the moral authority, to subsume those appetites and passions that interfere with our pursuit. It is not a matter of suppressing them. Rather, it is a matter of redirecting those energies toward new ends.

Again, it becomes clear that our practices must have 3L as their source. It is only from 3L that we gain the consciousness to see, for example, that shame *as a habit* can only exist on either end of a spectrum when conscience is absent, because from the perch of 3L our consciousness excludes unconscious shame. But jumping up to 3L requires just the kind of energy that our practices aim to contain, so how are we to reach 3L and gain the benefits of its oversight if we are still leaking the very energy we need to get there?

A cryptic answer to this question comes from the original practices of alchemy, where there was a saying: "It takes gold to make gold." 3L can oversee these practices, but when that energy is in short supply, we cannot stay in 3L for very long. So, until we gain proficiency, the oversight will be sporadic, occurring as brief bursts of conscience. But the process feeds on itself, and as we accumulate more energy, we will be able to stay present in 3L for longer and longer periods of time: It takes gold to make gold. For this process, even small amounts of 2L2 energy are enormously helpful as its nature is to flow in bursts in order to maximize its impact. Think of the orgasm, but also in more subtle manifestations such as when this energy is transmuted for intellectual discovery. Think of the aha moment. And it is just this kind of energetic burst that can propel our level of consciousness from 2L7 up to 3L, not unlike how electrons within an atom jump into higher orbits when there is a burst of energy available.

All of this goes to show just how crucial and just how central 2L2 energy will be to our progress. So now, what can we do?

The private practice best suited for 2L2 continence involves three parts. First, there needs to be an interval of sexual abstinence in every form, such that there is a building up of 2L2 energy. No guidance on the length of this interval can be given here because it varies so much, person to person, depending on just how leaky 2L2 happens to be.

The second part involves an individualized mapping of the habitual leaks between 2L2 and the levels where this energy is lost. We each lose 2L2 energy in ways that are unique to us. Some lose it to 2L1, where it results in a kind of sexual gluttony; some lose it to 2L3, where it results in some kind of predatory behavior; some lose it to 2L4, where it fuels the overexpression of emotions; some lose it to 2L5, where it fuels a kind of nonstop talking that is always looking for an audience; some lose it to 2L6, where it fuels speculations and conspiracy theories of every kind; and some lose it to 2L7, where it leads to fantasies, including posing falsely as a teacher, a guru, or even a healer! Some will lose 2L2 energy through just one of these leaks, but some will lose it through any combination of them.

The practice is to inventory one's own appetites and behaviors with the aim of simply observing what you discover without comment or judgment, as if these appetites or behaviors belonged to a stranger who you were trying to get to know. And as the central theme of 2L2 energy loss has to do with shame, be particularly attentive, curious, respectful, gentle, and loving. I repeat, do not judge what you discover. Your goal is to learn *what is*—to learn the truth through this science of interior experience in order for it to be clear where you are leaking 2L2 energy, so that this will not just be some intellectual theory, but a fact for you based on your own honest observations, and so your findings will be as they say "settled science."

The third part involves mapping out the links where you have unknowingly been successful in intending this energy to flow. Identify a pursuit of yours that you know intimately well, one that you pour yourself into and that gives you occasional flashes of insight that, over time, have yielded you some wisdom within this pursuit. Perhaps it is a sport, a craft, a creative endeavor, an area of intellectual curiosity, or perhaps a spiritual pursuit. It can be as "simple" as raising a child! It does not matter what the specific pursuit is, only that you can identify one where you have accrued some wealth of experience. Then, when you are engaged within this pursuit and in the same way as was given in the second part of this practice, observe without comment or judgment how the quality of 2L2 energy flows into your pursuit. Observe this as if you were privileged to witness how a highly creative person who was a stranger to you went about their work—be attentive, curious, respectful, gentle, and loving. In time, the spirits that feed on 2L2 energy that are strengthened through the extremes of unconscious shame will weaken by being recognized and being known. They disperse as one comes to value the conscious placement of 2L2 energy into a pursuit of one's own choosing, leaving less and less for one's default exchanges.

There is a public practice to 2L2 continence: no sexual contact without the presence of a mutually loving, mutually trusting, and mutually respectful relationship. Simply put, before engaging in any relationship that taps into 2L2 energies, ask, "Do I love X and does X love me? Do I trust X and does X trust me? And does X respect me and do I respect X?" But this simplicity bears the need for a thorough explanation.

Mainstream religions all put some strictures on sexual behavior, although little or no explanation tends to be given. From a sociological perspective we can identify the need to assure that any resulting offspring will be well taken care of and well raised, and from a medical perspective we can identify the need to limit the spread of sexually transmissible diseases. But our focus is on ways that 2L2 energy can be lost and how its loss can result in the loss of other energies that detract from our aim. Casual sexual contact outside of a loving, trusting, and respectful relationship is an absolute drain on 2L2. A few examples will make this clear.

First, let's take the most extreme case of sex without love, that of sex without consent. Within every culture, there is a value placed on a woman's virginity and a shame placed on those who have been raped. These are not intellectually derived values but instinctive reactions that cannot derive their real meaning from a Materialist view of human existence. It is only possible to understand their real meaning when the immaterial aspects of the sex act are taken into consideration—yet another concept that Western medicine finds absurd!

In its most common form with a female victim, there is a sense of deep violation that can be difficult to heal, although the practices given here can be of great help. Energetically what transpires? All sex acts poke holes in the 2L2 reservoirs of the partner who is penetrated. Each hole from each partner creates what amounts to a minor chakra, a point of coherence where, in the case of pregnancy, a new soul can enter and where the love of a partner who has poked that hole serves as an abiding source of energy. But without that love to fill that new opening, this minor chakra becomes nothing more than a hole where 2L2 leaks out, like a channel poked in an earthen dam. For more on this subject, I point the reader to the second book of this trilogy, *Letters to a Young Healer*, the chapter on sex.

Through the anastomosing architecture of 2L2, this leak drains the energies of 2L3, the source of one's will, and 2L4, the source of one's emotions, which flow in order to keep 2L2 full. It is why individuals who have been sexually violated and remain unhealed often lose their drive and develop a flat emotional affect.

Next, let's take the case of casual sex with many different partners. Each new partner pokes a new hole in the 2L2 reservoir, so even if there was consent for each occasion, the results are multiple leaks. In this case 2L3, the will, is not subverted because there was consent, so it suffers no loss, but 2L2 will be constantly replenished by the emotional energy of 2L4, resulting in a hardening, a jading of emotions, making it difficult for the quality of compassion to form in the right way and so working against our aim.

Finally, let us look at the results from the male side. First, imposing sex without consent requires a predatory and compassionless energetic structure that runs counter to our aim. Second, while casual sex with multiple partners pokes no holes in a man's 2L2 reservoir, the casual release of 2L2 energy is simply a direct drain on a man's supply. In addition, men who view multiple partners as conquests are channeling 2L2 into 2L3, resulting in a predatory mindset that has as its basis the character of arrogance, the single most efficient inhibitor of an atmosphere of healing.

Sexual union within the context of love, trust, and mutual respect can add to each partner's 2L2 reserves, or the act may be neutral or result in a temporary depletion depending on the energetics of each person and the circumstances of any particular union. But none of these possibilities run counter to our aim in the way that casual sexual behaviors do.

CHAPTER 15

2L3 CONTINENCE: THE ENERGY OF WILL

2L3 SERVES AS THE reservoir for our *will*. It occupies a position that is both the highest level of our instinctive center, 2L1–L3, which is externally coherent with S1, the spirits of our appetites, and it occupies the lowest level of our emotional center, 2L3–L5, which is externally coherent with S2, the spirits of our passions. As the highest level within our instinctive center, it has oversight and makes judgments for 2L1–L3. This directly impacts the coherences we are able to make with S1. With some level of intent, it provides us with a stable ego through which we interact, often through either relinquishing or affirming our power. Common examples of these interactions include student versus teacher, worker versus boss, or soldier versus commander. With more refined intent and sufficient energy, 2L3 can be the instrument for the healing energy of External

Qigong. But at its most conscious it becomes silent, surrendering oversight to 3L and making way for the higher-order spirits that give rise to true moral authority, a crucial element within an atmosphere of healing.

In the default state where 2L3 is least conscious, it leaks energy through the accidental S1 and S2 coherences that mark one or the other extreme end of a spectrum defined by the two faces of arrogance: tyranny or victimhood. With tyranny, the will is commandeered by spirits of greed, a striving for personal power, money, conquest, and a sense of superiority, where no one and nothing can be better or higher: *"I make the rules; I'm God around here!"* With victimhood, the will is relinquished to spirits of helplessness, hopelessness, and inferiority: *"This wouldn't happen to me if there really was a God."* I must be clear here: This is not to imply that there aren't situations in life that create real victims. That is a different subject. Here I am referring to victimhood as an unconscious habit of being through which one views the world.

Both of these extremes see a world devoid of any ultimate moral authority, and it is this that defines the nature of arrogance. Healing as a grace requires a channel to heaven, consisting of an abundant hierarchy of energies that have been specifically harmonized so that healing may flow through them. It is not worth considering any grace if we cannot first acknowledge a hierarchy of consciousness, a hierarchy of spirit that possesses a greater sense of truth, goodness, and beauty than we can ever imagine.

With arrogance, we can't imagine any such thing, and so, it is the single most effective means to inhibit the impulse of healing.

Recall this point that we covered early on: Arrogance led the Church to lay claim to knowledge of the material world, though it lacked any sense of what was needed to reach a real understanding of that realm. Arrogance has also led science to lay claim to knowledge of the immaterial world, though it lacks any sense of what it would need to reach a real understanding of that realm. Is it any wonder that healing has fallen into such disrepute? It's frayed like a rope in a tug-of-war, with each side pulling with its own manner of arrogance.

And so, it falls to each of us to root out our own arrogant tendencies, even small ones. Those place us into unconsciousness about our effects on others, and in that process our 2L3 energy is consumed by S1 spirits with an appetite for power and S2 spirits with a passion for arrogance. Sometimes we are followers, sometimes we are leaders, but our aim must be to temper our will with an intention of fairness and respect. In this way, we function in the middle of the spectrum and never fall into the least conscious ends where spirits of arrogance feast on our power.

But what benefits keep us content in either energetic extreme? On the one hand, there can be a sense of pride to having the strong ego that is typical in a tyrant-type personality. On the other hand, there can be a sense of militant entitlement coupled with a freedom from real responsibility that is typical in a victim-type personality. The difficulty lies in not wanting to give up the control that either of these conditions imply. In short, we must practice obedience to our higher aim and relinquish the control our ego feels through either of these two extreme roles. This isn't easy. As the Cistercian monk Thomas Merton once famously stated (in 1968's *Letters from Tom*), "Poverty is a cinch, chastity is harder but manageable, but obedience is a bugger!" And without a spiritual guide as Merton had, you've got to find the strength from within your own will, even as it may be weak through the loss of 2L3 energy. Once again, it takes gold to make gold.

The 2L3 practice has three parts. First, you face the difficult task of discovering instances where you have acted as the tyrant or the victim. This is difficult because we don't tend to view our actions in a negative light, and so it is common to call our behaviors by other, less unpleasant names. If you have a trusted friend, relative, or counselor who can be honest with you on matters such as this, you can get a jump start on the first part of this practice by asking for an example where that person has seen or felt you acting selfishly. Accept what you learn, but hearing about your behavior secondhand is not the same as having an experience or the remembrance of an experience firsthand. Also, because each of these extremes implies a relationship—a tyrant can't be a tyrant without a victim and a victim cannot be victimized without a tyrant—it will be important that if you are going to ask someone to help you with this practice, be extra careful not to choose anyone who you might be codependent with, as you will only benefit from a cleanly outside opinion.

In the second part, you've got to take what you have learned and examine it from the inside out. Even discovering a single instance from each end of this spectrum is like a gift! For example, have you ever taken advantage of a situation and struck a hard bargain that was a big win for you, but a bad deal for the other side? On the other end of the spectrum, have you ever played up an injury or an emotional slight in order to gain sympathy? In taking this inventory, it is important to do so objectively and without judgment; as we have discussed, bring your sense of attentiveness, curiosity, respect, gentleness, and love. You are trying to see what is, not judge what you see or change what you find. The value of this private practice is to prove to yourself, not as an intellectual speculation but as a fact of interior experience, under what circumstances and in what way you habitually lose 2L3 energy.

In the third part, you are to look within your history to any circumstance where you have made conscious use of 2L3: bargaining in good faith, showing fairness and goodwill, bringing value to others, not taking advantage when it would be easy for you to do so, or, on the other hand, asking for help that you may need without taking or implying any recourse to entitlement. In these kinds of circumstances, the arrogant spirits that feed on 2L3 energy will weaken as you intentionally use this energy before they can lay claim to it.

The public practice of 2L3 continence is a practical refinement of the Golden Rule: "Do unto others as you would have them do unto you," and the Great Commandment as cited in the first three Gospels: "Love God with all your heart, soul, mind, and strength and love your neighbor as yourself." It is taken from the philosophical teachings of the Christian mystic George Gurdjieff and is known as the exercise of "considering." Briefly stated, you are to find opportunities within your day-to-day life where, from your previous inventory, you know that your tendency would be to give life to arrogance by taking selfish advantage, in some subtle or obvious way. And in this new circumstance you are to make every effort to put yourself in the shoes of the person you are dealing with, seeing the situation from their point of view and at the same time see, feel, and sense your own internal state, but do not in any way succumb to it. In short, always externally consider and never internally consider.

Your goal in this practice is to put yourself into situations where you know in advance that it will take effort to resist your natural tendencies. Over time, as this effort becomes a habit and as such requires your awareness but no longer your attention, you will have succeeded in starving the spirits of arrogance lying in wait at the unconscious ends of your spectrum of 2L3 energy. And this in you, coupled with mastery of your 2L1 and 2L2 practices, creates intent, the conscious capacity of your instinctive energy essential for communing with the higher-order spirits of S4–S7. Intent is also foundational to one of the three being-states that must become stable for an atmosphere of healing: compassion without sympathy. And while compassion itself is more tied to 2L4, without the foundation of 2L1–L3, there is insufficient grounding to be able to offer compassion without getting helplessly drawn into another person's suffering.

CHAPTER 16

2L4 CONTINENCE: THE ENERGY OF LOVE

2L4 SITS AT THE confluence of two rivers of energy and is the reservoir of our compassion and love. But it is a reservoir that in its optimum state is more like a combustion chamber, where the two inflows are measured, metered, and rhythmically blended to produce a kind of fire. These inflows are the upward movement of our life energies from 2L1–2L3 meeting and comingling with a downward flow of either conscience from 3L or with greater internal coherence, from the higher-order energies of intuition, inspiration, and the revelatory states of grace. The result is the capacity to experience and offer a conscious kind of love that Thomas Merton referred to as "God's infinitely disinterested love."

In general, conscience enters this chamber as a small volume, the "still, small voice" spoken of in 1 Kings 19:12, compared to the larger volume of life energies, as conscience descending is like the rhythmic dripping of water off a leaf after a rain. With the higher orders of spirit, S5, S6, and S7, the admixture gains a higher proportion of this downward flow: first a trickle, then a stream, and by the time we get to the torrent of grace, we are at about fifty-fifty. That is, if we are in a state of conscious surrender and are receiving grace, then the center of our awareness will be in our hearts, in 2L4, and about half of our quality of awareness will stem from our own life energies and about half will stem from grace. This is in accord with what we know about Jesus and, by extension, what Christians aspire to: living in grace, both fully human and fully divine.

To further understand this, let us take an analogy from the world of the internal combustion engine. Within the cylinder of a typical car engine, a large volume of air is pulled in along with a much smaller volume of gasoline, in a proportion of about 94 percent air to 6 percent fuel. Then, at just the right moment this perfectly proportioned fuel mixture is ignited and the car is made to move. But in a high-performance drag racer, instead of gasoline the fuel is the more explosive nitromethane and it is mixed in a much higher proportion, usually around 50 percent air to 50 percent fuel, which yields a bigger punch to the wheels. Think of our life energies of 2L1–L3 as the air being brought into our 2L4 combustion chamber. Then if the fuel is conscience, we get an ignition like that in a typical car engine. But if the fuel is grace, the result is like racing fuel—our fire burns more brightly, and this can be a visible thing. If you encounter someone flooded by grace, there is an unmistakable brightness in their eyes.

This is the beauty of 2L4 and its physical counterpart, the heart. It is a rhythmic mechanism that brings energies together and transforms them into something of a higher order, and by this means love and compassion enter our world. But in its default state where 2L4 is least conscious, we lose its energy in one of two ways, neither of which contains a flame.

The loss happens at the two extreme ends of the spectrum that describes the inflows of these streams of energy. Near the center of this spectrum we have an upward flow of life energy meeting a downward flow of conscience, and from this configuration we experience compassion without sympathy, or a true compassion that has nothing to do with one's own needs or ego. In the exact center of this spectrum, we have an upward flow of life energy meeting a downward flow of grace, and from this configuration we experience love without possession, or Thomas Merton's "impersonal love." But at the two unconscious ends we have our two default states: *love without conscience* and *conscience without love*.

In love without conscience, we have a default state where the trickle of conscience bypasses 2L4 and instead flows into 2L3, the center of our ego. This yields all varieties of possessive love, such as jealous love, needy love, and suffocating love, and here we find passions such as an all-consuming sympathy. Earlier, we explored how compassion without conscience yields only a subjective love and how this is a common path for losing our emotional energy through a kind of gushing sympathy. The best descriptor for how we lose our 2L4 energy when we experience love without conscience is that it bleeds out of us.

At the other end of the spectrum we have conscience without love, a default state where the trickle of conscience gets bottled up in 2L6, the center of our thinking. This is a common thing in our culture, particularly among those who have been highly educated. There is a conscience in the mind, but not in the heart. This yields a lack of compassion, intellectual arrogance, a cold heart, and passions such as anger, impatience, and depression. Whereas in love without conscience the unconscious love can at least flow, in conscience without love, the 2L4 energy stagnates in its reservoir, often causing damage to the physical heart. Conscience without love has been a condition since biblical times, where mention is made, in chapters 33 and 34 of Exodus and in the book of Acts 7:31, of a "stiff-necked people" who resisted the Holy Spirit. The best descriptor for how we lose our 2L4 energy when we experience conscience without love is that it all dries up.

The practice for 2L4 continence first involves identifying which end of the spectrum is your default. Because 2L4 is an energy that only manifests when it is flowing in some kind of relationship, the bulk of this practice must occur within the context of some kind of relationship.

For those who tend to default to love without conscience, the practice starts by identifying a love relationship where you tend to get consumed by your feelings. Of course, people fall in love because it feels good. The point is not to deny good feelings, but rather to see if the quality of love flowing through you can be heightened to include conscience and perhaps even grace. When you find yourself immersed in a "swept away" experience, the experience serves as a cue for you to observe what is happening without making any effort to judge or change what you see.

In the beginning, understanding in this area will feel almost accidental, on its own and at random. A drip of conscience from 3L will intrude into your otherwise fully consumed 2L4 awareness. But with sufficient intent, this can become less random and more habit of being. How to encourage this? We must come back to our aim and wish to be a channel for an atmosphere of healing, a facet of the love of God. You must see this as a conscious choice. Either a loss of this energy flowing out of you in exchange for the pleasure of a consuming love or a gain in your experience of conscious love owing to the energies filling you from above. Then it is a matter of making a practice out of love without possession. This is a practice where you enter into a relationship where you expect nothing in return. The purpose of this practice is not to martyr yourself, as that is just another way to bleed out your energy. Rather, it is to make a conscious choice to put a selfless love into a relationship for the benefit on the other person and in this way to serve as a channel for God's love on Earth. This happens to be a key practice for developing an atmosphere of healing.

For those who tend to default to conscience without love, the practice of developing 2L4 continence is more circuitous. The key to undamming 2L4 appropriately without it defaulting to the opposite extreme is an undertaking that any psychologist will tell you is often quite complex. We will sidestep the psychological issues that may contribute to this being one's favored default state and focus on the narrower subject of addressing energetic flow.

At the outset, I want to acknowledge that if you tend to this as a default state, then congratulations for picking up this book and making it this far! So much of the territory that we have already explored involves a nonintellectual acceptance of conscious love. Simply making it this far demonstrates an opening for conscience to drip into 2L4. Nevertheless, this practice will focus on creating and enlarging that pathway for the fuel of conscience to enter the combustion chamber of 2L4, and to do this, we will start with relationships that are much, much simpler than interpersonal ones.

First, you must pick a level of complexity on which your practice will begin, as love exists on every level of complexity. Begin with a level that is emotionally easy and familiar to your experience. For example, if you love woodworking or have some craft that you can put your heart into, that can be a good place to start; it is not necessary that love be focused toward a person. Alternatively, if you have some workplace project that you are passionate about, that would also work. Moving up to higher levels of complexity, if you like to garden or take care of houseplants, then this can be the center of your practice. Or, if you like animals, you can focus this practice on tending to their care or training.

Regardless of the level you choose, the practice stays the same: In this relationship with a thing, a project, a plant, or an animal, have a goal in mind that ignites in you a passionate interest. Then pursue this goal with the overriding sense that you are going to bring as much quality into this work as you possibly can. No shortcuts, no compromises. And as you pursue this goal through this constant constraint of quality, you will meet with resistance. It may come, as an example, from the material itself—a piece of wood that will not cut easily, a project that meets resistance from other team members, a plant that won't grow properly, or an animal who won't cooperate. The practice itself is in this friction between your pursuit of quality and the resistance that you will meet. Confront that resistance with endless patience. Your ego will make efforts to intervene either through a tendency to pretend that these frictions don't exist or else by arrogantly dismissing them. Your practice is not to pretend and not to dismiss, but to remain steadfast in your pursuit of quality, not out of an ego wish to succeed, but out of a wish to have every step of the process occur within a mood of excellence, patience, and reverence. Here, we are turning the age-old philosophical question "Do the ends ever justify the means?" on its head. While you may rightly take satisfaction from whatever end result you derive, the end result is a secondary benefit to this practice. The primary benefit of this practice is all about what quality of means you are able to bring into the process. This practice will need to be repeated endlessly in life, moving up to higher and higher levels of complexity. By the time you reach interpersonal relationships, 2L4 will be burning with fire.

CHAPTER 17

2L5 CONTINENCE: THE ENERGY OF EXPRESSION

2L5 SERVES AS THE reservoir for our energies of expression. As such it has no mind of its own, but rather it is like a puppet that must be set in motion. On its own it can only express things out of habit, for example automatically repeating words, ideas, or stories that it has expressed countless times before. It sits at the junction of our emotional center and our thinking center, receiving input from both and responding to both. It can also serve as the means of expression of what can come through us when we become coherent with the higher-order spirits of intuition, inspiration, and the revelatory states of grace.

2L5 energy is spent whenever we express anything out of conscious choice including speech, writing, or any form of artistic expression. But outside of conscious choice we lose 2L5 energy through two opposite unconscious habits that are triggered by our emotional and thinking centers: unbridled expression and fearful repression. In the case of conscious choice, we open our 2L5 wallet and pay, while in the cases of unconscious habits, we are having our pockets picked! Alternatively, 2L5 energy is conserved when we consciously cultivate silence or when, through internal coherence, something higher expresses itself through us.

A central question of this energy has to do with our discernment of what is flowing through us. The ego is masterful at tricks! We may believe we are choosing to express ourselves in some conscious way when we may just be expressing something that feeds our ego, or we may be convinced that we are channeling some higher force when our ego is just acting spiritual. For our aim, we must be truthful with ourselves about what is flowing through us and not live in a world of delusion that inflates our ego while sapping our strength.

Let us explore the workings of 2L5 in more detail. In a state with some input from 3L, when there is some inflow of conscience, the energy that gives rise to our expression is edited or colored by what conscience deems to be remarkable. That is, of the thoughts and feelings passing through us, if these are just the usual things, nothing is deemed worthy of remark. But if some thought or feeling stands out in some way, it will trigger some kind of expression through 2L5, whether that be in the spoken word, the written word, or through some other kind of creative expression. When there is an alignment between our emotional and thinking centers so that they "speak with one voice," 2L5 serves as a vehicle for something higher to speak through us: intuition, inspiration, and the revelatory states of grace. It is here, for example, that words can heal.

But in its default state 2L5 loses energy in two ways. Without the higher editor from our conscience, an impulse from our ego and feelings (2L3–L4) or an impulse from our thoughts and imagination (2L6–L7) happily takes the reins. It triggers 2L5 to express without filter whatever we are feeling or thinking. At the opposite extreme, when 2L5 sits astride an unexamined conflict between an emotion or intellect around whether or not to express something, 2L5 energy devolves into 2L1 energy, fueling muscle tensions such as facial contortions and the clenching of the jaws. This was noted even in biblical times in the books of Matthew and Luke where there is mention of "wailing and the gnashing of teeth," where the mind awakens to what the heart has long ignored or suppressed.

It may seem contradictory for 2L5 energy to be conserved on the one hand when we consciously refrain from expressing ourselves yet lost on the other hand when we feel trapped in a thinking/feeling conflict that thwarts us from expressing ourselves. In both of these states, 2L5 is silent. But in the former, there is a conscious decision to ponder the experience, using the pressure of 2L5's wish-to-express as a motivator, while in the latter the conflict is simply repressed, causing it to devolve and spill out into a lower form of energy.

This brings us to the central question of 2L5 continence: Exactly what is getting expressed through this apparatus? Is it a thought or a feeling that out of habit or ego simply flows through us and gives us the pleasure of expressing ourselves? Is it the result of conscience making a feeling or an idea understood for a reason outside of ourselves? Or is it the result of a conscious surrender where something higher flows through us and becomes a help in ways that we may never fully understand? On its own, it talks and it expresses itself until it is all leaked out. If we apply intent through conscience, we can meter the outflow to serve our own purposes. And, if we can store enough of it, it can become internally coherent with other levels and then, without loss of 2L5 energy, something higher can express through us, and one form of higher expression is an atmosphere of healing.

So, how can we practice to minimize 2L5 leakage and put 2L5 energy in the service of our aim? First, we must observe what we express, and this is most easily accomplished when we are speaking. This is a more advanced practice than what has come before because our task is to see the nakedness of our expression in glimpses while we are expressing ourselves and not have this observation alter what we express or how we express. In most cases, this involves having our expression proceed automatically while we are bringing awareness up to our observer level of 3L, where we can see without judgment, emotion, or intellectual filter. Once again, this is not an exercise in vanity; we are not trying to see ourselves in order to admire ourselves or to "self-improve," but instead we need to see through the lenses of truth and objectivity. Can I observe if I am expressing myself just to blow my own horn, an impulse from 2L3? Can I observe if I am simply venting my feelings, an impulse from 2L4? Can I see if I am making small talk just to fulfill a social norm, an impulse from 2L5? Can I see if I am trying to make a rational argument, an impulse from 2L6? Can I see if I am acting out a role that is a fantasy, an impulse from 2L7?

Any of these impulses can be habitual or original, depending upon how automatic versus conscious we are in that moment. This brings us to the second part of this practice: observe in glimpses what is on autopilot and what is in the moment. Seeing in this way enables us to spend our 2L5 energy through our intent and not via an appropriation by forces that drain us.

The third part of this practice involves an exercise in pondering, an inner state known within the tradition of the Catholic Church as infused contemplation. It is a silent "being with"—holding a question, a wish, or a prayer in one's heart and being open to a higher order of knowing. We will apply this to an experience we already described: At some point you will find yourself in a conflict between speaking your thoughts and feelings or holding them back, based on your feelings or thoughts, respectively. In this state, by default, your 2L5 energy will start to devolve into 2L1 energy, which will manifest as some kind of physical tension. When you become aware of this, let it trigger in you an impulse from conscience to resist this devolution and its expression in any form. Instead, you are to use the pressure of 2L5's wish-to-express as a motivator to ponder the experience; not through any kind of rational problem-solving, but by bringing a measure of internal coherence to the junction of your thinking and feeling spheres, you will attract S6, the higher-order spirit of inspiration and creativity. From this state and your silent attentiveness within it, you will gain a seed of the reconciliation you seek. This is an ancient practice that goes back to biblical times. The interested reader is encouraged to study the apocryphal text known as the Book of Wisdom.

CHAPTER 18

2L6 CONTINENCE: THE ENERGY OF REASON

2L6 CONTAINS THE reservoir for our mental energy, known as *Shen* in Chinese medicine. In our modern culture, it is where the experience of our consciousness lies much of the time with the aim of acquiring and processing information. Mostly, our everyday awareness is immersed in 2L6's default exchanges with S3. These manifest as thought streams that we attract through our cultural background, family experience, education, and the idiosyncrasies of our personality. For example, when the default state of 2L2 pushes its energy up into 2L6, we have streams of hypersexualized thoughts and view the world through that lens. When 2L3 operates through its default state, we have streams of egocentric thoughts and view the world through that lens. When 2L4 is shut down, we have streams of compassionless thoughts colored with arrogance, and when 2L7 invents fantasies or lies, these descend into 2L6 and become patterns of such states as chronic worry, catastrophizing, conspiracy theorizing, or grandiloquence. By means of these thoughts, without our thinking we are leaking 2L6 energy all of the time. But here, we must make an important distinction.

As long as we are alive, there will always be thought streams in the background of our awareness, like a car sitting at a stop sign with its engine idling. It burns fuel, but not much. So, our initial efforts at 2L6 continence are less worthwhile when we concentrate on trying to stop the thought streams themselves, as this is akin to fighting the flow of a river. Rather, we accept these as a fact of life but aim to choose when we dip our toe into this river, hop in for a swim, or sit at the water's edge and listen to its roaring currents or sit back from the bank and ignore its sound. It is in this way that we begin to tame our experience of these thought streams.

Later on, when we gain continence of the other 2L energies that mix with 2L6, we can make headway in halting the flow of the river itself. But for now, we've got to focus our aim simply on not falling in, as we lose most of our 2L6 energy when we stumble head over heels into the stream without having any clue about how to swim. When that happens, we are consumed by the river and our 2L6 energy pours out of us. But it is not just happenstance that we fall in. Rather, in our default state, we can't imagine any place we'd rather be than thrashing around in the river. Consider the plight of little Freddy, a five-year-old in a candy store:

At the front of the store is a glass display that holds the candy that Freddy craves. But he can only gaze longingly, because there is glass between him and his quarry. But beyond the display is a counter with jar after jar of luscious candy and all within reach! Freddy becomes like a soldier at war. Without restraint he commandeers great handfuls of candy, shoving the sweets deep down in his mouth like a starved, wild beast, fearing his mother's wrath but driven by an irresistible force.

Just like little Freddy, we are driven to merge with an environment that in our default state is irresistible. So, to begin reclaiming our 2L6 energy, we've got to construct something like the glass display case that separates Freddy from his candy. This starts by recognizing that 2L6 is wired to accumulate information, and in its default state it exists in either of two extreme attitudes: in the conceit of "I know this," or the concede of "I don't know this." These habits of mind permit us to be as unconscious as possible in the face of legions of new impressions all coming at us, allowing only quick snap judgments. This keeps us immersed in a kind of mental triage, with no time to come up for air and certainly no perspective to see that we are thrashing about in a river.

These states sit at the least conscious ends of a spectrum whose center point is the question "What is here for me to learn?" This is the point from which our experience is one of curiosity without arrogance and without rush to close off deeper understanding. It is the point where what mixes with 2L6 is a bit of energy from 2L7 and a drip of conscience from 3L, and it is from here that higher levels of knowledge can be known. From this state the wish for this kind of opening brings the focus of 2L6 away from the polar ends of conceit or concede where the river roars loudest and nearer toward a quiet center where we find curiosity and a love of truth that we call "integrity to be in accord with the highest kind of love."

The practices for 2L6 continence involve three parts. First, we can begin by making an effort simply to listen to the flow of our thought stream from the point of view of the riverbank. In other words, we are to observe our internal talking without getting immersed or consumed by it. Instead, we treat it as the babbling of a beloved relative who may be getting a bit senile; we listen to them prattling on, but we don't get too attached to what they are saying. Second, when a new impression comes in, try to see if your own tendency is to pigeonhole it through conceit or concede, resisting either tendency to instead make an effort to be open to a deeper level of knowing. Third, making daily efforts of our First-Order practices will, on its own, build the glass case that gives us the separation from our thought stream and paves the way for a better relationship with our own inner streams of thought. And this, coupled with the practices to gain continence in the other levels that often agitate 2L6, will ultimately allow you to quiet down the river within you.

CHAPTER 19

2L7 CONTINENCE: THE ENERGY OF IMAGINATION

2L7 CONTAINS THE reservoir of our energies of imagination. It is what gives us the ability to have abstract thoughts not tied to strict rationality. Above its default state, it receives a constant drip of conscience from 3L. Indeed, it is our closest window to conscience, and through this we can experience intuition, inspiration, and wisdom. In its highest state, if we are open to a belief in a reality above what Materialist science recognizes, a door can be open to the higher revelatory graces, a door that doubt otherwise nails shut.

For this highest level, we must also count on an upward overflow of the energies of 2L1–2L6 to supplement and stabilize our conscious experience in 2L7, and for that we must first achieve continence on many other levels. But we still need continence in 2L7 itself in order to experience imagination through the lens of consciousness. So, how is it that we lose 2L7 energy? As with the other levels, we lose it to one of two default states that sit at the unconscious ends of our spectrum of imagination. On one end we find the internal construction of fantasies, and on the other end we find the external projection of lies, both of which drain us of 2L7 energy and profoundly affect our atmosphere.

In terms of fantasies I am not talking about the inventions of the novelist or the dreams of one who is striving to succeed. Those may be fantasies, but they are created with great care and a great deal of consciousness. I am talking about unconscious fantasies that are the construction of imagination colored by 2L1 prowess, 2L2 sexual longing, 2L3 retribution, 2L4 idolatry, 2L5 fame, or 2L6 elitism—pipe dreams without discipline or desire for anything more than a familiar and pleasant escape. These kinds of fantasies burn through the precious fuel of 2L7, leaving nothing for more conscious pursuits.

In terms of the external projection of lies, I am not, for example, talking about the craft of a trained actor who makes a conscious effort to project a character distinct from their own inner self. That projection may be a lie, but it is deliberately created for a conscious purpose. Also, each of us often needs to craft a persona appropriate to our role in society where it may be inappropriate to share the more personal levels of our being. But to shed light on the kinds of unconscious lies that spill 2L7 energy, let us revisit some earlier concepts and put these concepts in a new light.

Previously we have used the concept of a cable lock to visualize an alignment of 2L levels, and we have also used the concept of the seven major chakras spinning like hurricanes with open eyes creating a channel for conscience or grace. Let us now use a different concept to visualize this channel of aligned and harmonized reservoirs, less a visual image than an interior experience: that of integrity and how it touches on what kind of atmosphere we emanate.

When there is a lack of integrity between and among our centers, they each act in a different way but all at the same time. People experience us through our words, our actions, or our presence, and our atmosphere is what conveys our presence. When our centers each speak with a different voice, our presence emanates a mixed message that others experience as cognitive dissonance, a term used by psychologists. For example, if I tell you that I love you but at the same time I am shaking my head, then this would confuse you. Or, if I tell you to relax and settle down, but if I myself am anxious and flailing my arms around, then you would likely become even more nervous. Confusion and healing do not go hand in hand. This type of lying drains 2L7 because there can be no upward flow of 2L1–L6 energies while they themselves are not of one voice.

This harkens back to the authors of the Bible. Not only were their words considered sacred, but they also could not simply phone in their beliefs in an off-the-cuff kind of way. They had to be authentic so that their words, their deeds, and their presence all lined up. When there is this internal coherence among all of the 2L levels, we become capable of channeling the revelatory states of grace including an atmosphere of healing. But if 2L7 leaks energy to unconscious fantasies or to these kinds of lies, the door cannot open to these higher-being functions.

What practices then can we use to minimize this spillage? In terms of fantasies, we must attend to instances when we are unintentionally harboring them. The simplest way is to begin looking for recurring daydreams that we default to as an escape from our present moment and then to make an effort to abstain from those for some interval in order to build up 2L7 energy. No guidance can be given on the length of this interval of abstention because it varies so much, person to person, depending upon how leaky 2L7 happens to be.

In terms of lies, we have now come to the most subtle and difficult of all of the Second-Order practices. Indeed, religious devotion is a time-honored tool for purging oneself of these hindrances to grace. These practices are subtle and difficult because the lies that affect our ability to have our levels all speak with integrity and in a single voice exist within the traces of unconsciousness that remain among our 2L1–2L6 levels. We must be relentless in shining our spotlight of attention on these remaining dark corners. This was difficult even for St. Paul, who in Romans 7:19 stated, "For I do not do the good I want to do, but the evil I do not want to do—this I keep on doing."

In Judaism there is the ritual of *chametz* carried out the night before Passover that speaks symbolically to what this practice requires. Following the admonition from the book of Exodus 13:7 that "no leaven shall be seen in your possession and no leavening shall be seen throughout all of your borders," the faithful go throughout their homes carrying a candle, a feather, and a wooden spoon. The candle is to illuminate all the dark corners where there might be found a crumb of leavened bread. When found, the feather is used to sweep it into the wooden spoon from which it can be discarded. But when all the dark corners have been seen and swept clean, the wooden spoon itself is burned, because it itself had been contaminated with the leaven.

It is with this same spirit of tenacious, conscious purposefulness that we must make a practice out of rooting out all that interferes with our integrity. But in this, we are not alone. Going back to the saying of the alchemists, "It takes gold to make gold." Even imperfect integrity cracks open the door for grace, and it is through small revelations that we gain the strength and the vision for rooting out the most hidden corners of our being.

It is appropriate at this point to bring up the topic of false healers. In this category also go false teachers, self-proclaimed gurus, and religious leaders who are unfaithful, overly materialistic, or predatory. Here we see how the imagination of 2L7 can be put to uses that go against our aim. False healers create a narrative about themselves that they may even come to believe, but that does not line up with their actions, interests, or capabilities. There is imagination but no conscience. For our purposes, we must always strive at least to bring a bit of 3L into the functioning of 2L7 and better still if we can hold our alignment sufficiently open to allow in the states of grace.

One further point, in both the construction of fantasies and the projection of lies, our experience is never in the present moment. In fantasy we are far away from "right here and right now," and in a lie, we take a step back from reality as the lie acts like a filter on our being present in the moment. So, any effort to be authentic in a deep and thorough way makes it hard for fantasies and lies to play through us. And no revelatory state of grace including an atmosphere of healing can exist except in the immanent present.

Perhaps the single most helpful thing is to cultivate a persistent attitude of *reverence* in everything and everyone you attend to. Be patient with yourself and with the work you have before you and with the people you have around you. I have found no better advice on this practice than what has come down to us from the seventeenth-century Lay Carmelite Brother Lawrence, who spent his life in a priory as a cook and as a sandal maker. His approach was chronicled in the book *The Practice of the Presence of God*. It presents an approach to *reverence*, which is the keystone to creating and maintaining an atmosphere of healing. I close this chapter with five quotes from Brother Lawrence (taken from the 1895 edition by Fleming H. Revell Co.):

"We ought not be weary of doing little things for the love of God, who regards not the greatness of our work, but the love with which it is performed."

"Prayer is nothing else than the sense of God's presence."

"There is not in the world a kind of life more sweet and delightful than that of a continual conversation with God; those only can comprehend it who practice and experience it."

"People seek methods of learning to know God. Is it not much shorter and more direct to simply do everything for the love of Him? There is no finesse about it. One only has to do it generously and simply."

"It is not necessary to have great things to do. I turn my little omelet in the pan for the love of God."

CHAPTER 20

THIRD-ORDER PRACTICES: EXCHANGE

IN OUR FIRST-ORDER practices, the goal was to strengthen our awareness and our intent. We began to correct what in our culture is an overemphasis on having our awareness locked within our thinking apparatus, and we cultivated habits of attending to the more subtle expressions of interior experience. In our Second-Order practices, the goal was to attend to the energies of our organization that give rise to our qualities of interior experience and work to keep those energies from being lost due to unconscious habits. When these energies can be made to accumulate, we become capable of varying degrees of internal coherence that allow us to manifest, for example, compassion without sympathy, love without possession, and a reverence that imbues our actions and presence. When internal coherence can be brought to our entire organization, we gain an integrity to be in accord with the highest kind of love. This said another way is a channel for grace, a form of which is an atmosphere of healing.

In the introduction, I described healing as an art with science behind it, analogous to the art and science of jazz improvisation. As with jazz, there is a science behind the art, and in the case of healing, I have described this science in terms of what life is and what consciousness is. In turn, this foundation makes it clear what practices we've needed to develop this art. By analogy to jazz, First-Order practices are akin to learning the musical scales, and Second-Order practices use those scales to play musical sentences rather than just sequences of notes. Third-Order practices involve playing tunes with other musicians in order to develop the skills to publicly perform. Fourth-Order practices would then be the performances themselves, and for us, Fourth-Order practices are our way of being present in order to create and maintain an atmosphere of healing.

For our purposes, Third-Order practices are our chance to develop our internal coherence from experiences that only happen when we are engaged with the world around us. It is one thing to close your eyes and meditate and gain a sense of inner experience. It is something else to open your eyes after meditating and maintain your inner alignment when confronted with the manifestations of the world. And it is yet a third thing to gain feedback from interactive practices so that you can honestly assess if you possess a skill, an alignment, or a capacity—or if you are merely fantasizing that you do.

Almost anything can become a Third-Order practice provided that the activity is done with intent, reverence, and a wish or prayer that the experience will help us toward our greater aim. These are the devotional practices that become rituals of daily life, dress rehearsals for the prayer, the service, and the presence that maintain the conditions for an atmosphere of healing.

All Third-Order practices share some key elements: There must be some repetitive aspect to it that can be made into a meditative ritual, there must be some element in it that serves as a check against fantasy, there must be the development of some skill that can lead to ever-greater degrees of mastery, and there must be some opportunity for feedback from other people so that the practice won't only exist in a bubble. We may interact with most but not all of these practices in any of three ways: We may participate in the practice itself, we may be a student of the practice with all of the rituals of learning, or we may be a teacher of the practice with all of the rituals of teaching. Any of these three interactions may equally qualify as a Third-Order practice. Because so many different things can work as a Third-Order practice, I can only give examples and specify how these practices can be of help. Feel free to substitute your own as long as these criteria are satisfied.

Music

I have used jazz improvisation as an analogous art to the art of healing, so it ought not to come as a surprise that the mastery of a musical instrument can qualify as a Third-Order practice. The mastery of an instrument is itself an exercise in intent, strength of awareness, self-patience, fortitude, and the development of a musical ear. The daily practice can be like a meditative ritual: We immediately get feedback in our ears if we hit the wrong note, and there is an endless road toward mastery. In playing for others, we get feedback on if we are able to move people with our playing or not, and there are ample opportunities for learning, performing, or teaching.

Art

One of my earliest experiences with a Third-Order practice was in the art studio when I studied life drawing. It is a time-honored tradition in drawing and painting to have a nude model posing in various postures and to render anything from quick sketches to complete works of art. The setting, the implements—the paper and charcoal or canvas and paint—and the gathering of the students for a common purpose all set the stage for a meditative ritual. We immediately get feedback through our own eyes if we manage to create a drawing that reproduces accurate contours, holds the same scale throughout, and captures something of the mood or character of the model. But for our purposes there is something more. Through the practice of life drawing, one gains an additional anchor to the here and now of held muscle tensions, postures, and attitudes. It is 2L1 consciousness rendered objectively as a complement and reinforcement to one's own subjective interior experiences. And in one fell swoop it develops internal coherence between 2L1 body awareness, 2L3 intent, and 2L5 expression. There is an endless road toward mastery, and if there is a teacher or if there is a culture of group critique, we get feedback from others to help us to see how our work affects others.

Craft

In the first two books of this trilogy, *The Charm Carver* and *Letters to a Young Healer*, I put much emphasis on crafts, whether they involved the charms that Simon carved, the bread that a baker made, the cleaning that a cleaning lady performed, or the weavings made by the Moon Lake Woman and later by Madeline. Craft accomplished through intent, strength of awareness, and integrity to be in accord with the highest kind of love can in and of itself manifest a simple atmosphere of healing. The objects or foods created under these kinds of conditions become coherent with S4-level spirit of prayer, and we have the possibility of inviting spirit in according to the principles established by Dr. Tiller's research with his intention-imprinted electrical devices or, among the faithful, through the veneration of relics, the sanctification of spaces, and the transubstantiation of the Eucharist. With craft not done assembly-line style—where there is a production mode mentality and an empty heart—but with craft done with a sense of ritual, a sense of sacredness, a wish for mastery, and a willingness to learn from one's mistakes and accept the feedback of others, there can be a practice that is as close to sacredness as any Third-Order practice can be. Recall the words of Brother Lawrence at the end of chapter 19: "It is not necessary to have great things to do. I turn my little omelet in the pan for the love of God."

Sacred Dance

Within this category I include the martial arts practices first mentioned in chapter 13, Tai Chi Chuan, but now we will focus on its sister practice known as Tuishou or "Push Hands." It is a practice performed between two people who each try to establish a root, meaning finding a footing that they cannot be moved from and at the same time trying to find an unyielding place in their opponent from which to push and uproot them. A similar martial arts practice includes the Japanese discipline of aikido and the more physically demanding sport of judo. While it is beyond the scope of this book to detail these practices, they each satisfy the criteria of a Third-Order practice in that they are highly ritualized, there is a path toward mastery, there is immediate feedback if you have not been able to hold your root, and you can serve as a participant, a student, or a teacher.

Sport

The development of a talent in any sport can easily be a Third-Order practice. The ritual of practice is there, and the feedback—did the ball go where I aimed it to go?—is immediate. There is an endless opportunity for mastery, and there is the feedback from line judges or referees that keep our versions of reality honest. And, of course, there is ample opportunity to be a participant, a student, or a coach. A particularly valuable aspect of having sport as a Third-Order practice is that it can be an ongoing lesson in having one's ego (2L3) in balance. Sport can be an exercise in winning at all costs, and losing will seem a failure to the ego. But as a Third-Order practice, sport becomes about continuous self-improvement that can only come about in concert with a strong opponent. This was instilled in me at a young age when I studied judo. In that sport, there is a bow to one's opponent before and after a match, signifying the honor of honing one's skills through the competition with the other. Winning was always secondary to this, and so it must be in one's inner attitude for sport to be a Third-Order practice.

Service Work

The giving of service, when done through a generous heart and a real commitment to grow and improve, is a Third-Order practice with value beyond price. It is a potent introduction to our main aim, which is a very particular kind of service. My own introduction to the practice of service work came as I was working my way through college and began waiting on tables. I highlighted the value of this in *Letters to a Young Healer*. To begin, service work tends to be a more physical, in-your-body kind of activity than the thinking that goes on in Western science education, and so it serves as a useful counterpoint. Second, it is highly ritualized. Third, there are skills to master that you can always improve upon and you get feedback in the form of tips that indicate either the quality of the job that you did or just how little valued certain patrons treat the help—which is a wonderful lesson in humility.

Other forms of service work that would equally suit the bill include volunteering of any kind. It could be in an animal shelter or a soup kitchen. The venue matters little, only that the situation and the setting permit you to turn your service work into a Third-Order practice.

CHAPTER 21

FAITH, SCIENCE, AND HEALING

IN SEPTEMBER 2018, a new medical, nursing, and physical medicine school opened up in Nutley, New Jersey, as a branch of Seton Hall University, a Catholic, faith-based school of higher education. The Interprofessional Health Sciences campus was a joint venture between Seton Hall and Hackensack Meridian Health. At the inauguration, Cardinal Joseph W. Tobin, the archbishop of Newark, gave an address where he said, "I think the unique feature of this partnership between a leading health system and a faith-based university is to prepare women and men for those moments when the hands reach their limit." (See NJ Spotlight News website, September 18, 2018.) And so it is that the expectation in our culture is that faith and all that goes with it enters the health-care equation at the point where science comes to an end.

I corresponded with Cardinal Tobin, and he was clear that his words were not meant to prioritize science over faith while in the arena of healing, but it is only honest to acknowledge that this is where our culture of health care stands. In the introduction, I addressed the downside of this from the standpoint of those in the healing professions. Now let me share with you what I have come to know on the basis of a study I performed on my own patients that was published in volume 46 (3) of *The Journal of the American Dental Association* in March 2015. I surveyed patients who traveled an average of about four hours each way to come to see me, in order to determine why they found it necessary to make such a distant trip for their care. The answers were organized into one of three categories: "clinical skills," "office atmosphere," and "traits of character," and the analysis showed a neat ratio of 1:2:3. That is, only 17 percent of the responses spoke to skills with clinical procedures, while 83 percent spoke to how the office "felt" and how these patients perceived me in ways besides my skills in clinical treatment. It was sobering to realize that 83 percent of patients' reasons for traveling almost 8 hours, round-trip, for their care had nothing to do with what I did, although those factors clearly created a foundation, but everything to do with how I am and how my office is. For these patients, it was less what I did than it was how I was and how my office was that caused them to travel so far to see me.

The benefits of faith enfolded into the strictures of Western medicine are significant. Through the acceptance of spirit and a hierarchy of complexity—the Great Chain of Being—we come to understand that our own structure is united with an unknowable world that maintains our existence on every level. And through an alignment that each of us can master, our being may serve as a channel for an atmosphere of healing, for higher-order spirits to mend what has become broken. These benefits are starting to be recognized by some who are currently on the fringes of Western science as they probe the boundary between matter and spirit and find in this interface the phenomena of consciousness, not directly probe-able but apprehend-able through a science of interior experience. And in this we have the beginnings of a reconciliation of science and faith from their schism 500 years ago.

In our world of science and technology, there is an epidemic of inattention. Ask any elementary school teacher who has a few decades of experience and you will quickly learn that lesson plans are now measured in short intervals of minutes compared to how things were before cell phones, video games, and social media. Our brains are now programmed from a young age to grow bored if things are not exciting all of the time as our world has grown more and more mechanized by the "efficiency" of technology.

In health care this has led to a crisis, not a crisis of treatment but a crisis of care. This is especially true for anyone who has an unusual condition that requires more than a standard six-minute examination and more of a doctor's or nurse's attention than the pigeonholing of a diagnosis or the recitation of standard, template-like answers to questions. Health care has become a machine and health-care workers its components, all designed to streamline treatment, make it more predictable, and "leverage technology" to make the system more efficient. This scientific mindset is ideal for a factory building automobiles, but it ignores that part of a patient's care that was cleaved off from science and left to the Church at the Council of Trent. There is no easy fix for this as our health-care system is like a huge locomotive hurtling down the track at high speed. Any effort to slow it down, let alone making it change tracks, is a gargantuan task.

But anybody who deals with someone who is sick or suffering—a physician, a nurse, a hospital chaplain, a friend, a mother, or a father—anyone can in just a small and private way offer a bit of solace, a bit of comfort, and through practices presented here, one can offer even more: a channel for the grace of healing. What is needed is an understanding of what healing is, which is a reharmonization on various levels of complexity within something that is alive. But this implies a need to understand that life itself consists of a series of levels of complexity, each with its own degree of consciousness, and where these levels interact in extraordinarily complex ways. But that implies a need to understand what consciousness is, which is the foundation of all levels of complexity and a "something" that will forever escape our five senses and all of our technology.

Through a science of interior experience, we can come to know a bit about our subtle structure, and through various practices, we can create alignments that permit us to channel higher powers that are healing to those within our small and private worlds. You must cultivate a particular quality of intense presence into each and every moment and make a ritual out of all that you do, but never, never must this ritual be something empty. The reciting of words, even words of prayer, done in a rote way as a habit of repetition, does not bring healing near. Healing comes from being entirely present, and the science of healing is a science about learning specifically how to be entirely present with a particular aim, a particular intention, and a particular wish or prayer.

It is a matter of taming one's appetites, passions, and thoughts. It is a matter of not losing energy to unconscious habits. It is a matter of assembling alignment after alignment so that they each form a link in a chain, a lock with the tumblers all lined up, an open channel: for intuition, inspiration, and the revelatory states of grace to descend from above—all in the service of healing. The states of grace are hard to put into words as within grace there are no words. As St. Teresa of Ávila put it in chapter 8 of her "Relations," from *The Life of St. Teresa of Jesus*, "When all the faculties of the soul are in union . . . the will loves more than the understanding knows, but the understanding does not know what the will loves; the memory has no power of thinking, nor are the senses awake." But on the way to grace we find inspiration and intuition, and gaining a sense of the interior experiences that accompany these states helps us understand how the practices that we've laid out create conditions for something higher to come through us. For an example of inspiration, we take an analogy from the world of business, and for an example of intuition, we take an analogy from the world of jazz improvisation.

Think of each of the levels on which we can become consciously aware, which we have called 2L1–3L1, and imagine each of these as individuals sitting around a conference table with 3L1 at its head. It's a meeting and there is a question on the table. 3L1 then asks around, and each level must speak to the question or be disciplined so as not to speak out of turn and so as not to change the subject or take over the meeting. Furthermore, there is mutual respect among the members for everyone's opinion, with no one participant claiming priority or superiority to any of the others except to 3L1. Each level speaks with a voice carrying its own wisdom and experience so that the inspired answer to the question will have the considered input from each and every participant.

Now imagine this scenario from the world of jazz improvisation, where 2L1–2L7 are notes on a piano derived from just a single octave and played in the left hand, forming the rhythm section or bass line, and 3L is an octave's worth of notes played in the right hand and sounding a melody line. In jazz, the fingering of the lower octave notes creates their own little melody. Each is important for the overall effect, and no single note is meant to stand out; they are designed to blend and create a feeling that the musician wants to convey. The voicings played in the right hand form a song over the bass line with everything happening in real time.

With inspiration there is time to consider and time to reflect. With intuition as with grace, whatever happens, happens now and in the moment.

Our primal life energy must not be depleted through exhaustion or fear. Our sexual energy must not be depleted through adventurism or purged through shame. Our energy of will must not be depleted through an arrogant tyranny or victimhood. Our emotional energy must not be depleted by unconscious love or conscience without love. Our energy of expression must not be depleted through unbridled expression or fearful repression. Our mental energy must not be depleted through the drowning in one's thoughts or through the tyranny of our logic. And our imaginative energy must not be depleted through the harboring of habits of fantasies or lies. Each expresses opposite states along seven individual continua. Energy leaks along these unconscious edges in the same way milk spills over the edges of a slightly tipped saucer. But if the saucers can be steadied, energy can accumulate in each of these, and with that comes the chance for a channel, one through which grace can descend. There is much we can do to "clean house" as it were, to bring all of these internal aspects into alignment and into tune. And with that comes something new: an emergent coherence of the qualities of intent, strength of awareness, and an integrity to be in accord with the highest kind of love that together create a new way of *being*, a way that creates and maintains an atmosphere of healing.

The Bible never promises a cure. In fact, in John 16:33, we learn "in this life, you will have tribulation." But in the twenty-third Psalm, we learn "though I walk through the valley of the shadow of death, I shall fear no evil, for thou art with me." The promise is the *presence* of God and in any given circumstance; we cannot possibly know to what degree or extent healing may come. But presence of the right sort is a very big deal. Consider Jesus healing the blindness of three different men. In Matthew 9:27–31, he uses his touch, in Mark 8:22–26, he uses his spittle, and in John 9:6, he mixes his spittle with the dust of the ground and applies this mud as a poultice. In every case, he is healing with his presence; the tools of his trade were simply details. We are not masters of the art of healing as Jesus was, and we are not even saints. But how would it be in our current age of Western medicine if drugs, surgery, and other forms of therapy were simply the details? There can be physical healing, like the woman with the hemorrhage who, through Jesus's mere presence, was made well, or Anne Theresa O'Neill, whose lymphoma was healed through prayer and the intercession of the future saint, Elizabeth Ann Seton. Or there can be a healing of spirit.

From time to time, a patient like Susan will come into my practice. She sat down and a flood of grief came out of her. I have been working within my current office space for over thirty years, and it has come to resonate with the intentions that I express there, day in and day out. This is nothing extraordinary as the spaces we each occupy eventually mirror our atmosphere in the same way as the walls of an old church hold the intentions of prayers. My space is quiet and feels emotionally safe, and it is in this environment that patients feel the freedom to unburden their hearts. They are not asking for me to problem-solve or to offer platitudes, only to be present to their suffering so that they can feel heard.

I put my hand on Susan's shoulder and listened as deeply as I could. I was "holding space," a term from popular psychology that implies creating an emotionally safe space in which a person may express whatever they need to express without fear of reprisal, challenge, or embarrassment. But within the context of the art of healing, holding space takes on additional levels of meaning. Through the practice of compassion without sympathy, I remained anchored in the present without being swept away by Susan's plight; after all, how could I be of any help to her if I began grieving with her and then needed *her* for support? Through the practice of love without possession, I held a second level of space, the open channel between each of my levels, so that I might be open to intuition, inspiration, and the revelatory states of grace. Third, through an attitude of reverence without end, I held open the possibility of something higher and more sacred entering into the moment; as St. Paul stated in Romans 8:25, "If we hope for what we do not see, we wait for it with patience."

But to be clear, in that moment I was not reviewing a mental checklist of these levels or inspecting myself to see if I felt open. Those speak to the science that is behind the art in the same way that a jazz pianist does not review music theory or fingering technique while in the moment of crafting an improvisation. With healing as with any art there is a time for the science that justifies all the necessary practices. But when it is time for the art, it is time to just *be* in the moment, *being* dependent on all that practice that came before it. Assembling these levels into a coherent whole is never easy, in the same way that climbing a mountain is never easy. But as with climbing a mountain, if you have developed your muscles and your experience, the climb becomes *familiar*, and in this regard, it becomes a habit of effort.

After a time, Susan's crying stopped and, in the silence that followed, grace appeared. First, she offered an unnecessary apology for her emotional display, but then a second silence came, and then when she spoke, there was a drop in the register of her voice and a calmness overtook her. And she came to see a different world, higher than her grief; all was just as it had been, yet nothing was the same. The pain remained but the suffering, at least in that moment, was vanquished by the grace of God.

It is never for us to know on what level or levels a healing presence may affect an ill or suffering person. All we can do is to bring an atmosphere of healing into the here and now and hold open the door for grace. The details of healing will always be contained within the same mystery that stopped the hemorrhage of the woman at Jesus's gathering, 2,000 years ago. Our understanding of the science of healing and our practice of the art of healing cannot pry at that mystery, but through our understanding of consciousness, we can come to know how we may assist in bringing this mystery down to those around us, and in this way, we are each helping to dry a tear in the eye of God.

FURTHER READING

THE FOLLOWING READING LIST is meant to assist those who have a particular interest in furthering their intellectual understanding of some of the concepts presented in this book. I reiterate a caution that I gave in the introduction: My wish is not for this book to serve as a jumping-off point for ever more intellectual pursuit, but for the interested reader to apply the knowledge and the practices provided here in order to develop their *being*. That being said, there is much good in the following recommendations.

- *Medical Miracles: Doctors, Saints, and Healing in the Modern World* by Jacalyn Duffin
- *Physicians' Untold Stories* by Scott Kolbaba, MD
- *Galileo's Error* by Philip Goff
- *Vibrational Medicine* by Richard Gerber

- *Quantum Reality* and *Faster Than Light* by Nick Herbert
- *Science & Human Transformation* and *Conscious Acts of Creation* by William Tiller
- *The Synchronized Universe*, volumes I and II, by Claude Swanson
- *Transcendent Mind* by Imants Barušs and Julia Mossbridge
- *Supernormal* and *Real Magic* by Dean Radin, PhD, et al.
- *Healing Words*, *What Is Consciousness?*, *Recovering the Soul*, and *One Mind* by Larry Dossey, MD, et al. In addition, I highly recommend Dossey's peer-reviewed journal *Explore: The Journal of Science and Healing*
- *Science Set Free*, *Science and Spiritual Practices*, and *The Presence of the Past* by Rupert Sheldrake
- *Is Consciousness Primary?* and *Expanding Science* by the Academy for the Advancement of Postmaterialist Sciences (www.aapsglobal.com). In addition, this is a great organization to join if you have an interest in staying on the cutting edge of the next scientific revolution.
- *Cymatics* by Hans Jenny
- *Views from the Real World* by George Gurdjieff

- *In Search of the Miraculous* and *The Psychology of Man's Possible Evolution* by Peter Ouspensky
- *Aquinas's Shorter Summa* by Thomas Aquinas
- *The Graces of Interior Prayer* by Augustin Poulain
- *The Interior Castle* by St. Teresa of Ávila
- *The Seven Storey Mountain*, *Letters from Tom*, and *Contemplative Prayer* by Thomas Merton
- *The Practice of the Presence of God* by Brother Lawrence

INDEX

A

D

E

F

G

H

I

J

N

O

P

Q

R

S

T

U

V

W

Z

ACKNOWLEDGMENTS

I'D FIRST LIKE TO acknowledge the decades-long support I have personally received from Larry Dossey, MD, a man I hold in high esteem for his life's work of publishing rigorous science on the subjects of consciousness and healing; the groundbreaking research of Dr. William A. Tiller, PhD, Professor Emeritus of the Department of Materials Science and Engineering at Stanford University who was, in my opinion, the first to lay out testable hypothesis on the nature of consciousness, intentionality, and healing; and the Academy for the Advancement of Postmaterialist Sciences for being a gathering place for those interested in this particular scientific revolution, still in its infancy. I'd also like to acknowledge all of my patients who over the years have allowed me the privilege of practicing my craft of dentistry while at the same time gaining, through my interactions with them, a real sense of what healing can be.

The underpinnings of my understanding of consciousness, attention, and how one's being can be grown I owe to my encounters with Pierce and Barbara Wheeler, William Segal, and Michel de Salzmann—proponents of a teaching referred to by their teacher, George Gurdjieff, as "Esoteric Christianity" or simply as "The Work."

Three individuals have been uniquely helpful in shaping the direction of this book: Larry Dossey, MD, the executive editor of *Explore: The Journal of Science and Healing*, who encouraged me to write it; Brent Bauer, MD, the director of the Program on Integrative Medicine at the Mayo Clinic, who first suggested that I make explicit what the previous two books in this trilogy merely implied; and Mary Ann Steiner, editor (retired) of *Health Progress: The Journal of the Catholic Health Association of the United States*, who having read *Letters to a Young Healer*, pointed out how my treatment of this subject was in accord with the inner struggles of those women and men in Catholic medical practices who toil daily to reconcile their faith with scientific medicine. The input from these three and their respective fields of science, healing, and faith guided my structuring of this narrative in a way that I hope will move these fields closer to reconciliation.

In addition, I'd like to acknowledge a number of individuals who have been helpful in developing the final form of this book: Peggy Wills for validating the theory and practices presented; Catarina Mako, BCC, ThM, DMin, director of Pastoral Care,

Hospital of the University of Pennsylvania, for reenforcing the sentiments of Mary Ann Steiner and advocating that this book be sure to speak directly to faith-based spiritual counselors, chaplains, and the clergy, and for her assistance in titling; and the entire support team at Greenleaf Book Group: Justin Branch, Lindsay Bohls, Lindsey Clark, Jordan Smith, Jeffrey Curry, Chelsea Richards, Corrin Foster, Evelyn Sher, Sam Ofman, and a special shout-out for the extraordinary design and artwork of Brian Phillips, who was able to take my ideas and rough sketches and translate them into artistic and informative images.

Also, this book would not have been possible without all that I learned about the practices of Tai Chi Chuan from my teacher, Master Don Ahn, and all that I am learning about jazz improvisation from my piano teacher, Dave Frank. Also invaluable has been the help of my two office managers Pam Michaluk and Suzanne Crouch, who made sure that whenever I was not treating patients, the door to my private office remained closed, affording me the quiet time and space that I needed to write.

A book loaded with new ideas always needs its first group of readers who are up for the challenge, and I have been blessed to have had these in abundance. A special thank-you to those who not only read the early manuscript but who also took the time to write such touching endorsements: Larry Dossey, MD; Irina Weil, MD; Allen Wells, BA, BD; Caterina Mako, BCC, ThM, DMin; Robert Kandarjian, DC; David Kramer, BA, MA; Fr. Charles Bouchard, OP; John Harrington, DC; Heather

Turner, PT, ATC, IMT; Donna Dimino; Amy Celento; and Hari Kaur Khalsa.

Finally, I am grateful for the support, quiet wisdom, and extraordinary photographic portraiture supplied by my wife, Mary.

ABOUT THE AUTHOR

DAVID SHUCH is a writer and a dentist, practicing in northwestern New Jersey. He is the author of three other books: *Doctor, Be Well: Integrating the Spirit of Healing with Scientific Medicine* (2003), and the two books that comprise the trilogy completed by this title, *The Charm Carver* (2005) and *Letters to a Young Healer* (2018). He is a longtime practitioner of Tai Chi Chuan and is a student of improvisational jazz piano. He resides near his practice with his wife and their companion animals.